THE
COUNT

By

RALPH DUTTON

With a Foreword by
OSBERT SITWELL

Illustrated from Photographs by
WILL F. TAYLOR *and others*
and from Drawings

THIRD EDITION, REVISED

1 WEST WYCOMBE PARK, BUCKINGHAMSHIRE (*circa* 1765)
By Robert Adam and others

*Detail of a Painting
by Algernon Newton*

FOREWORD

By OSBERT SITWELL

The English Country House is a delightful and informing book, full of interest, and will give pleasure to numerous readers. Mr. Ralph Dutton, indeed, is the perfect guide—No, not guide, but a friend with whom to walk round all these lovely places. He unfolds for us the widest panorama, studded with houses amid green trees; houses that are all different and all fascinating. For great as is his learning on this and kindred matters, he never treats country houses purely as *objects*, dead things left behind by previous generations, but he makes them the exquisite and appropriate shells of various manners, various methods of living: this infuses the house of which he is discoursing with a new charm.

But then, it is obvious that he brings to his subject a real love of it, all too rare in the author of such a book. The public, it is true, usually presumes, without any adequate examination of the premises upon which it bases this belief, that if an author writes of his particular subject he needs must love it. . . . On the contrary, the exact opposite is often the truth: he is more often than not actuated by a most bitter and intimate hatred, a blind grudge against it: this monster, as he sees it now, to which he has devoted so many wasted hours, about which he knows all that there is to be known, about which he has consumed so many reams of paper, scratching at it with an angry, if hypocritical pen. After this fashion, too, I apprehend, do the grim bands of museum officials hate the objects under their care. A similar loathing inspires them as they look at the precious objects of glass or china or bronze, these substances, brittle or enduring, to which their entire lives have been offered up; from which they can only escape as broken and bitter old men. . . . But unlike these, our author talks of his subject, English houses, with affection, and as if visiting these halls, examining their furniture and associations, were, as the accompanying illustrations so aptly prove it should be, one of the joys of his life.

Certainly, after enjoying his book, the reader will understand a thousand matters which had puzzled him before, and to which he had doubted whether he would ever find a clue. It will tell him what the people in these houses ate, how they felt, what they said, as well as what they looked like.   In this the book, although a comprehensive guide to actual architectural fashions, is indicative of a new approach.

Alas! how curious it is that these works of art only begin to obtain a wide appreciation when they are on the verge of being destroyed. . . . What country houses of any size, one wonders, can hope to survive the next fifty years? . . . And, indeed, as I sit writing these lines in an old house, I recall that two great houses in the neighbourhood have been dismantled and gutted within the last few years.

OSBERT SITWELL

ACKNOWLEDGMENT

THE Publishers are under much obligation to the owners who have so kindly given facilities for photographing their houses, but it should be clearly understood that their inclusion in this book does not mean that they are open to the public. Particulars of those houses that may in normal peacetime be visited, including those belonging to the National Trust and under the guardianship of the Society for the Protection of Ancient Buildings, H.M. Office of Works and other public bodies are contained in the author's *English Country Houses Open to the Public*, and James Lees-Milne's *National Trust Guide—Buildings*.

The majority of the photographs have been expressly taken for the book by Mr. Will F. Taylor. In addition to these the Publishers must acknowledge their gratitude to Messrs. Aerofilms for Figs. 45 and 74; Mr. Hugh Cholmondeley for Fig. 47; the late Mr. B. C. Clayton for Figs. 11, 12, 121 and 127; the proprietors of *Country Life* for Figs. 38, 61, 67, 81, 82, 112 and 128; the British Council, for photographs by Mr. J. Dixon-Scott for Figs. 15, 27 and 109; Mr. Herbert Felton, F.R.P.S., for Figs. 13, 32 and 131; Messrs. F. Frith & Co. for Fig. 120; Mr. Ewing Galloway, of New York, for Fig. 116; Vera and Humphrey Joel for Figs. 51 and 75; Messrs. Knight, Frank & Rutley, Ltd. (photograph by Messrs. Millar and Harris), for Fig. 113; Midland Air Services for Fig. 98; The Topical Press Agency for Fig. 93; and Mr. A. J. Woodley for Figs. 14 and 24.

Figs. 17, 18, 25, 30, 39, 53, 57, 58, 64, 68, 76, 77, 78, 79, 80, 83, 87, 88, 91, 92, 94, 97, 104, 105, 107 and 129 are from the Publishers' collection. The illustration on page 12 is from a drawing by Mr. Brian Cook and that on page 110 is based on the Ordnance Survey Map with the sanction of the Controller of H.M. Stationery Office. The illustration and plan on page 42 are reproduced from *The Buildings of Sir Thomas Tresham*, by J. Alfred Gotch; the plan on page 79 is reproduced from *The Architecture of Robert and James Adam*, by Arthur T. Bolton, by permission of the author and of the publishers, *Country Life* Ltd., and that on page 55 by permission of the *Builder*. Thanks are also due to Mr. Algernon Newton for his kind permission to reproduce the painting used as frontispiece. Fig. 110 is from the collections of the Victoria and Albert Museum, South Kensington.

CONTENTS

2   HADDON HALL, DERBYSHIRE: a Corner of the Hall (*circa* 1300-1330).   The Screen is of the mid-15th Century

3 KEDLESTON, DERBYSHIRE : the Central Feature of the South
Front. Robert Adam, architect, 1765

THE ENGLISH COUNTRY HOUSE

CHAPTER I

INTRODUCTORY

No nation has the love of country life more firmly implanted in its character than the English, and it is an unfortunate chance that few, if any, European countries possess a larger proportion of urban population. This apparent inconsistency is accounted for by economic needs still, it seems, in process of fulfilment—a process that is gradually depleting the countryside of its population and swelling the towns to unwieldy and frightening proportions. Nevertheless, the English town-dweller generally clings to some illusion of the country in his urban exile, almost as desperately as does the colonial administrator (so we are led to believe) to his dinner-jacket in the remote outposts of Empire; and manages to lend what verisimilitude he can to the charms of semi-detached suburbia by giving his house at least a rural-sounding name. The Pines, Acacias and Chestnuts run a close race for popularity with the resounding names of famous country seats: Blenheim, Chatsworth, Sandringham; Rosebank, Brackenwood, Briarlea tell their own story of hearts throbbing for the open spaces; Normanhurst, Holmcroft, Saxonmead are a somewhat ambiguous fruit of the varied philological root-stems of the English Shires. The crowd of black-coated workers around the window of any city flower-shop, the immediate success of any garden suburb, are further proof, if proof is needed, of an emotion that is perhaps one of the most amiable of those that beset the English temperament.

One has not to dip deeply into social history to find that the house or cottage in the country has always been, as now, the chief domestic goal of the urban worker. In the more spacious life of the ruling classes it was invariably the country house that was the home, the town house the temporary and little-considered lodging. The richest architectural effort was, except in rare instances such as the Adam Brothers' London houses and the Woods' terraces and crescents at Bath, reserved for the country; and however much we may deplore

B

the passing of the several private palaces of London, it is perhaps for the agreeable open spaces afforded by their gardens that we should shed our most substantial tear. For each of them had its garden, each was, in effect, a modest country house in town. But the English counties still abound in incomparably finer specimens of domestic building than anything that London has had to offer.

Out in the country, there can be few who can ignore the appeal of the traditional village group. The Hall or Manor, the church, the rectory, the clustered cottages in the local vernacular: these elements variously grouped, in their setting of smooth fields and old trees, create an aura of domestic peace and well-being that even the events of the last quarter-century have hardly succeeded in disturbing. The village, that small microcosm of English life which, until the passing of the nineteenth century, remained so compact, so self-sufficient, was but one of the cells building up the body of the state; with the break-up of the private estates, the gradual disintegration of rural life, the body is starved of one of its most vital sources, a steadying bulwark of sanity is disappearing from public affairs. Most people have experienced the feeling of sadness and incompleteness in a village in which the "big house" is derelict, demolished or turned into an institution. It is not only the sight of a devastated park, grass-grown drives and broken fences that depresses us, but a feeling deeper and more spiritual, a sense of intangible loss which probably even the village socialist will share. The English are a sentimental race, and, apart from economic considerations, there is enough in the spectacle of a stricken system, grown sweet and familiar by usage, to make the most insensitive among us mourn.

For until the end of the nineteenth century the passing years had brought little change to the village community. The Tudor manor-house had perhaps given way to a more ambitious mansion, the Church had undoubtedly been drastically restored, and possibly with misguided optimism as to the growth of the congregation, enlarged during the active years of Victorian ecclesiology. At about the same time the landowner, with a sudden realisation of his duties, may have altered the appearance of the village by the building of some unlovely but more commodious dwellings; occasionally, in an access of benevolent zeal, he may even have pulled the village down outright and replaced it, as Samuel Whitbread did in Bedfordshire, by a "model village" complete with

4　HOLCOMBE COURT, DEVON (mid-16th Century).　Notice the tall Entrance Tower

5　WROXTON ABBEY, OXFORDSHIRE : the Entrance Front (late 16th Century)

hollyhocks, a parish pump, and an old-world air. But on the whole change was reluctant and tardy. The keep or fortified manor, presiding like a protective hen over the mud cottages clustered around it, gave way to the unprotected mansion, with lawns, orchards and a fishpond; but still the cottages crowded round, not so much for protection as to take their share in the complex workings of the manorial farm. Thus the "big house" often remained in intimate proximity to the church, where the generations of its owners rested under monuments often forming in themselves an epitome of smaller English craftsmanship; to the cottages, where John Stoutlook, Ralph Jolibody and Robert Litany, succeeded in their time by David Noakes, Robert Holdaway and Jeremiah Mundy, kept a cautious weather eye cocked upon the Hall, whose "justice room" dispensed the penalties for village misdemeanours, whose ample kitchens provided the plenty of the boon-feasts at times of harvest and sowing.

Sometimes, as prosperity and ambition came to the owner, he would desert the older house and build himself another, larger and more magnificent, in the centre of its own park tamed out of the shaggy tangle of the waste lands and far from the sights and sounds of village life. The examples of this development about England are numberless, but one of the most charming is at Cothelstone in Somerset, where the Tudor manor-house, little church and great barns and buildings of the adjacent farmyard lie in close and neighbourly proximity within the village, while half a mile away, in dignified seclusion beneath the wooded slopes of the Quantocks, lies the Georgian Cothelstone Park. The Early Renaissance magnates were the first to feel the desire to isolate themselves from the rural world around them; the majority of vast houses of that period, Wollaton (42), Longford (50), Burghley, were set down lonely within immense parks, though Hatfield, as the air photograph (45) shows, was and remains closely identified with the village. Not often did dislike of even the remotest contact with the humble reach such a pitch of phobia as with the sixth Duke of Somerset, however, who insisted that before he set out in his coach the Sussex roads should be cleared by outriders lest he should be subjected to the gaze of the vulgar. It was an ironical coincidence that his house, Petworth (7), begun in 1689, like Cirencester Park which dates from early in the following century, was built upon the ancient site of the one it replaced, and so close to the little town of which it forms the hub that its entrance is in the main street; while on the garden side the park sweeps into the distance for miles.

The architecturally sterile years of the Civil War and Commonwealth left the country gentry (and there were never more of them than at this time) with a veritable mania for building and planting, the results of which often remain to delight us to this day. Mrs. Celia Fiennes, in the course of her lively and observant tours of the English counties, seldom passed a day without inspecting some "newbuilt" house, or one in course of construction; while those who were not building were at least enlarging their parks or, like Colonel Hutchinson during the Interregnum, diverting themselves "in the improvement of grounds, in planting groves, and walks and fruit-trees, in opening springs and making fish-ponds." With the eighteenth century came the boom in agriculture due to improved methods of farming, and the movement for the enclosure of common lands—lands which had been at the disposal of the villagers from time immemorial for pasturage, wood-gathering, snaring—to the great profit of landlords and farmers, if not of their dependants. Country-house incomes often swelled to more than substantial proportions at this time, largely, it must be admitted, at the expense of the now landless class of agricultural labourers, whose general plight reached perhaps its lowest depth of misery and degradation at the period of the Napoleonic Wars. But despite the callous attitude of many landowners, there were still some who could combine a solicitude for their tenantry with a practical acceptance of the new theories of farming. Of such, quite early in the century, was Thomas Coke of Holkham, great-uncle of the famous Coke of Norfolk, who enclosed, drained and planted many hundreds of acres of salt marshes on his Norfolk estate with profit not only to himself but to his tenantry.

For the architecturally minded, the eighteenth century was a period of endless activity and stimulation. Many of the recipients of large incomes now found themselves in occupation of rambling and uncomfortable houses built for their ancestors under the Tudors, without beauty in their eyes or even convenience, and now no doubt largely derelict as a result of the many disturbances of the last century. What could be more natural for a man of quality than to utilise a swelling income in rebuilding the ancestral home, particularly now that his position in the county was apt to be judged by the magnificence of his house and the extent of its park?

Hence many a substantial classical pile laid out in the grand manner with no false modesty as regards ostentation, in the midst of a thousand acres of rolling parkland. Another incentive was the rivalry of neighbour with neighbour, and there were many parallel cases to that of the young Lord Stawell of Somerton who, succeeding on his majority in 1690 to twenty-eight manors in Somerset, set about building what he vowed would be the finest house in the county. An immense structure, 400 feet long and 100 feet wide, began to take shape amid embryo terraces and gardens; but alas for vain boasts! Before it was even half completed Lord Stawell died, already financially crippled by his ambitions and with only two of his twenty-eight manors remaining to pass on to his impoverished heirs. Indeed bankruptcy as a result of over-building has been a peculiarly English failing through many centuries; more families, perhaps, have been ruined by this amiable mania than by any other fashionable extravagance.

Among the rich at least, the century was a halcyon period of taste. These gracious well-planned houses, so appropriate in every detail of furnishing and decoration, formed a perfect domestic setting for a breed which, if one can credit the canvases of Gainsborough, Reynolds and Zoffany, could achieve beauty without effeteness and dignity without affectation. However high their culture and cosmopolitan their outlook, these men and women seldom seem to have lost the precious capacity for living country lives. Never, like the aristocracy of France, did they aim at bringing the life of the town to their country houses; never quite, despite the dangerous and difficult dawn of the nineteenth century, did their class become so remote from the labouring masses as to find itself, as happened across the Channel, suddenly overwhelmed by a surge of bucolic hatred. On the contrary, the smaller squire, from Mr. Western to Sir Walpole Crawley, was often wont to prefer the company of the village taproom to the elegancies of polite society: a red-faced, hard-riding rustic, speaking the dialect of his county and hardly distinguishable from his own tenant farmers save in his tacit assumption of authority as a member of the ruling class: the gentry. It was an assumption that spread beyond the confines of Park or Hall, as far as Westminster and Whitehall; for throughout all this period, and even to well within living memory, English political life has had a "country-house" flavour very much its own. The principal credential of the would-be politician, whether sedate Tory or sprightly Whig, was a social eligibility mutely recognised by his equals and respected by his inferiors. As a convention this undoubtedly excluded from the business of government some of the astutest talents and brightest spirits of the times, yet in the long run it proved a not unsatisfactory system, though probably to a great extent responsible for that reputation for gentlemanly hypocrisy which the English have never lost in the councils of Europe.

But perhaps the most important contribution which the country house and its owners made to English culture was in the encouragement of the arts. Architecture, for which the English have always shown a natural talent, was easily diverted by the Reformation from ecclesiastical to secular needs, while under the same aegis sculpture, painting and design, fostered by the importation of foreign craftsmen, reached an ultimate standard of somewhat tardy achievement that made the later English house unsurpassed in quiet domestic beauty. Many architects owed their early training to the patronage of the great; the Duke of Northumberland sent John Shute to study in Italy in 1550 to the great advantage of English taste; Lord Pembroke sent Inigo Jones on the same mission half a century later; William Kent was the companion of Lord Burlington on his European travels. But patronage was not confined to foreign excursions, for many country houses would hardly have seemed complete unless they kindly sheltered some artist or writer, struggling for fame or already wearied with Parnassus. One thinks of Turner at Petworth and Pope hobbling among the groves of Cirencester; of the mingling of culture with government and government with wit at Stowe and Wilton; of what for a brief time Newstead meant to Byron and his friends. Whatever the motive, there can be no doubt that much English talent could never have found maturity without the patronage and leisure that was the gift of the country house.

But there was another side to the medal. Few architects when designing these buildings gave more than a passing thought to the housing of the servants. The kitchen, it is true, received its share of attention and was usually light and spacious—far too spacious, in many cases, for the diminished households of to-day. But the sleeping accommodation was meagre in the extreme; the men-servants were crowded together in windowless rooms in the basement, while the

6 THE VYNE, HAMPSHIRE: the Entrance Front of this very famous house, built in the 16th Century and altered, it is said by John Webb, in 1654

7 PETWORTH HOUSE, SUSSEX : the West Front, as painted by Turner from across the Lake. Begun in 1689, possibly from the designs of a French Architect

maids were assigned to equally restricted quarters in the attics behind the parapet. The arrangements at Mereworth Castle in Kent, as originally designed by Campell about 1720, were by no means exceptional; here there were only four upstairs servants' rooms in the shallow pent of the porticoes, each lighted by a small round window. And the discomforts of the household staff were probably less than those of the outside servants and labourers, who were often left to exist as best they could in the smallest and most decayed of cottages. One has only to look at some graceful eighteenth-century lodge, which seldom comprises more than two small rooms, to realise what at this time must have been considered exceptional accommodation, as such being probably reserved for some specially favoured retainer. Fortunately these lodges are often twin, so that the space intended for two families can now sometimes be made to suffice, though barely, for one.

With the turn of the century, however, came a sudden access of solicitude for the life of the labouring poor; instead of banishing the village workman from sight and mind in a tumbledown hovel, a picturesque *cottage orné* would be built as a new feature of the park, ousting as an object of interest the pagan temple of half a century before. No longer would the purpose of a walk be to take tea in the Temple of Venus or Jupiter; rather the lady bountiful would set out, with her basket of food of a suitably simple variety, to brighten the lives of the grateful indigent. This turn of fashion appears very clearly in contemporary novels such as those of Maria Edgeworth. Even the indolent Lord Glenthorn, in *Ennui*, was subject to "hot fits of benevolence" towards his starving tenantry.

"Benevolence" of the sort increased as taste declined, until the latter reached its low-water mark a little past the middle of the nineteenth century. Now no longer was the rage for building confined to the large landowners; all classes began to feel the zest for bricks and mortar, with the result that all over the country new scarlet edifices, blatant without, dark and gloomy within, began to make their appearance in such numbers that they have come to be a familiar feature of the English landscape. Unfortunately the "grand manner" had by now been completely abandoned; the houses might be vast in scale but they were almost always niggard in detail and planning. Equally in planting the "touch" was lost. The sweeping plantations advocated by Brown and Repton

gave way to arid clumps of Scots or Austrian pine placed
with little regard to the lie of the land or the suitability of
conifers to the district.

Never, however, had the country-house life been more
popular; never had it been maintained on more lavish a
scale. Despite the frequent cries of ruin, money was never
perhaps so plentiful as in the full-flowering of the Victorian
age; and it may be that in time to come the delightful sense
of ease, opulence and security that lulled the generation of
our great-grandfathers may, by association, and by the dis-
appearance of some of the worst monuments, tend to blind
us to the shortcomings of a lamentable period of taste, and
almost reconcile us to the allurements of Victorian Tudor
and Victorian Gothic.

The builders of country houses at this and other ages were
able to excuse unjustified extravagance by the thought that
at least these sumptuous piles, these finely timbered parks,
would be enjoyed by their descendants for generations to
come. Nowadays, alas, the old certainty of tenure has departed,
and the owners of large houses and estates must frequently
feel that they are the last of their family to enjoy them; few
certainly would be bold enough to embark on extensive
schemes of planting with the idea that their grandsons would
be able to appreciate them in their full maturity. Whether
or no the country house, as the centre of a community and
of an estate, is doomed to certain extinction it is difficult to
say; but undoubtedly we are more conscious of declining
than of rising families, though perhaps the progress of dis-
intregation is slower than it seems.

Every architectural book published during the last century
or more exhibits a certain complacency; at last, the authors
cry, domestic architecture has abandoned its bad old ways
and seen the light. The heavy aldermanic classic has been
discarded for a romantic Gothic; the latter in its turn has
been superseded by a more sober style deriving from the
finest indigenous examples of Christian Architecture. A few
years later, how narrow it seems to draw inspiration only
from the half-fledged efforts of national Gothic while ignor-
ing the weightier achievement of Northern France! And then
Venice, Lombardy, Spain, why should they be excluded?
(Only Germany, the original home of the Goths, seemed
unreasonably to lack appeal.) So the note of self-congratu-
lation persisted through good taste and bad, though mostly
through bad. Whatever the value of contemporary achieve-

8 THE MOOT, DOWNTON, WILTSHIRE: a delightful "middling" house of *circa* 1690

9 WIDCOMBE MANOR, BATH, SOMERSET (*circa* 1730). The House groups very
pleasantly with the little Church

ment, we would do well, perhaps, to keep to tradition and end here on a note of quiet optimism, fixing our eyes rather upon the high-lights of domestic building to-day than upon the rows of shoddy little dwellings that stretch for miles to disfigure the green verges of our bypass roads.

CHAPTER II

THE ENGLISH VERNACULAR

(*Circa* 1066 to 1550)

THE conquest of Saxon England by the Normans was a comparatively gradual process. The Battle of Hastings was followed only after an interval of several months by the fall of London, and this uncertain hold on the capital had quickly to be consolidated by the erection of a fortress on the propitious site of a Roman castle near the banks of the Thames. Not until this building, which was to develop into the Tower of London, could provide a certain degree of security did the Conqueror enter the town with his main body of troops. On Christmas Day 1066 William was crowned King of England in the Abbey at Westminster. But his title was still an empty one, his precarious domination spreading only over the south-eastern quarter of the country.

Wider conquest was followed by the hasty raising of further strongholds, but the Normans' building was not confined to aggression and defence. As early as 1070 Lanfranc, the first Norman archbishop, started work on the construction of a cathedral at Canterbury based on the Conqueror's own church of St. Stephen at Caen, and nine years later Bishop Walkelin embarked on his vast scheme at Winchester. These buildings had a twofold purpose in being raised to the glory of God and to impress upon the Saxons the superior power and culture of their new masters.

The century following the Conquest was too disturbed for any advance to be made in domestic building, but towards the end of Henry II's reign the erection of fortified manor-houses began. Not many of these early structures have survived, but enough remains to give a fairly clear picture of their general plan.

The manorial system of land tenure had been widespread throughout England for several centuries before the Conquest, though free settlements had also existed in parts of the country. Under the new *régime* the manor became the accepted unit of government. The Saxon theyns were replaced by William's followers, the more adventurous of whom were given *carte blanche* to carve out for themselves new estates in distant and

10 WINCHESTER CASTLE : the Great Hall (*circa* 1230)

12 OAKHAM CASTLE, RUTLAND : the Interior
of the Great Hall (*circa* 1180)

11 BOOTHBY PAGNELL, LINCOLNSHIRE : an
only Stone Manor-house of *circa* 1180

unreclaimed parts of the realm. The Conqueror's more influential adherents were rewarded by liberal grants of existing manors, some of which they, in their turn, passed on to subordinate officers. Riches, so far as they existed in eleventh-century England, were accounted in terms of manors; a great lord might own literally scores of them; a lesser one might live on, and farm, a single estate.

The nucleus of each manor was its house, in which lived the owner or his resident bailiff. This at first consisted merely of a hall with very minor dependencies; around it were grouped farm-buildings and sheds to form a courtyard, and beyond were the open fields and meadows of the common farmlands and demesne, the latter being the home farm whose produce supplied the needs of the lord and his household. The hall would generally be the only building of stone, which accounts for its occasional survival when every trace of the outbuildings (which were of *pisé*, or rammed earth, thatched with straw) has vanished.

During the earlier centuries at least, the demesne lands, and those of the few freeholders or *sokemen* who had retained their property through the rigours of the Conquest, were mingled apparently indiscriminately with the ploughed strips of the "unfree" tenants, or villeins, each of whom was allowed the produce of his own "virgate" of some thirty acres in return for services on the demesne and certain dues in kind. The whole estate, in fact, with its meadows, woods and pastures, was worked on a complex system of communal husbandry by which the villein was allowed to extract a bare living from the soil in return for "customary" duties to which he and his family were bound in perpetuity by feudal ties. While the villein could be bought and sold at his lord's caprice like any beast of the stall, it was seldom in practice that he was separated from the land on which he had been reared; and despite what might appear to modern eyes the many tyrannies of the system, he existed for the most part in considerably better circumstances than the average agricultural labourer at the close of the eighteenth century. At the same time, his conditions could hardly be called ideal according to modern standards. His hut consisted generally of two compartments, one for the family and the other for the beasts when brought in from pasture on the common waste. But we may hazard that, on a cold winter night, family and beasts alike would draw together around the open fire of dung or peat for warmth.

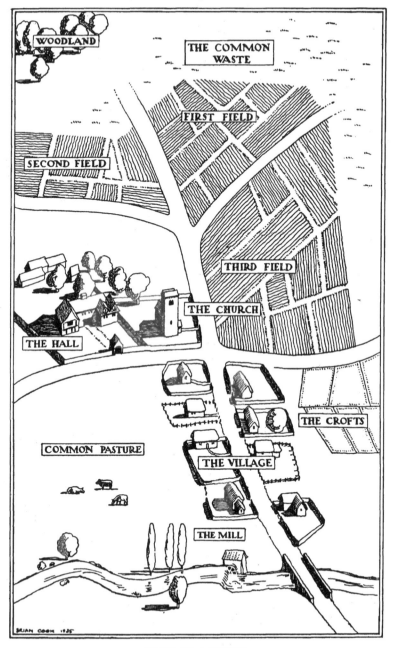

PLAN OF A MANOR

Such were the precursors of our later farmhouses and cottages. As for the manor-houses, it was seldom that the owners of large estates inhabited any one of them for long at a time. While in theory the lord of the manor was in complete control of his estate, administering its affairs and dispensing justice in his own court (where, incidentally, from early times the jury was composed of villeins), in practice these duties were generally carried out by a bailiff, often with the help of a reeve appointed by the tenants to control their affairs. Lack of supervision led to frequent hardships among the *personnel* of the manor, and complaints against unjust stewards were not rare. It was a more satisfactory arrangement when the lord maintained a continual progress from one of his manors to another, followed by his retinue and a packhorse train loaded with his few essential household goods, such as tapestries and glass windows. When the resources of one manor were depleted, the party would move on to the next.

As regards the buildings themselves, the Normans knew of only one method of spanning a large floor area, and this they adopted both for their ecclesiastical structures and for the more ambitious of their manor-houses. The Norman hall thus assumed much the same form as the church, with a nave separated from side aisles by pillars supporting round arches. It was only in this way that a large quadrangular space could be covered.

The finest domestic example surviving of this construction is the hall of Oakham Castle in Rutland (12), built by Walkelin du Ferrers about 1180. It measures internally 65 feet by 43 feet, and the beauty of the design and fineness of the detail make it one of the most splendid works of the Transition from the Norman to the Early English style. A double line of pillars with elaborately carved capitals supports the arches on which rested the beams of the roof, but the latter has been entirely renewed. An Inquisition of 1340 mentions, in addition to the hall, four chambers and one kitchen which have disappeared. There is no sign of a fireplace, and the fire must have been in the centre of the hall, with a louvre in the roof above for the escape of the smoke. The building was not fortified, and the lovely double lancet windows, divided by shafts, would have been most unsuitable for defence. The whole site, however, was surrounded by a bank and moat, and it indicates an improvement in the state of the country that these were considered sufficient guard against molestation.

The building commonly known as King John's House at

Warnford in Hampshire is another but very ruinous example of this form of structure, though it dates from a good many years later. The pillars are 25 feet high, and there are clear indications that a wooden screen, which became an invariable feature for the centuries following, was erected across the west end of it.

The great hall at Winchester Castle (10), built on the same plan, was begun in 1222 and completed about twelve years later. It is far larger than any previous domestic building, being no less than 111 feet long and 55 feet wide: the aisles are formed of clusters of slender shafts supporting pointed arches which span a space of 19½ feet. Forty years had seen a surprising development from the single pillars and round arches of Oakham. The double lancets with transoms, and a pierced quatrefoil above, are the earliest extant examples of this style of tracery, but somewhat similar windows occur at Stokesay Castle in Shropshire (13), which dates in part from a few years later. During the next century (*circa* 1340) windows of the same form, but with lighter and more graceful tracery, were incorporated in the design of the great hall at Penshurst Place in Kent.

Simultaneously with these halls, a more modest type of house was making its appearance, consisting of a simple parallelogram divided into two storeys, the lower a stable or cellar, the upper a living-room. A good example of this arrangement is the so-called Norman House at Christchurch, Hampshire, which dates from the second half of the twelfth century. Here there is a basement lighted by narrow slits in the walls, while on the first floor is the hall, a large room with windows on three sides and a fireplace surmounted by a circular chimneystack. The floor, which has disappeared, was probably of wood, and the roof open-timbered. The manor-house at Boothby Pagnall near Grantham, which probably dates from a few years later, consists similarly of an undercroft and upper chamber, here approached by an outside staircase (11). Another simple form of early house was a long single-storied building, primarily a stable, of which one end was boarded off for living. Here it may be added that the term "hall" was by no means confined to the principal room of a fortified manor-house, but might equally well be applied to the living-room of a cottage. Since it was always the most important part of the building, however, it is hardly surprising that the whole house often came to be called "The Hall."

13. STOKESAY CASTLE, SHROPSHIRE. The South Tower (in the centre) dates from *circa* 1291; the Hall from *circa* 1240; the timbered Gatehouse and the Timberwork on the right from *circa* 1620. The whole group forms the most complete surviving example of the medieval fortified manor-house in this country

14 LOWER BROCKHAMPTON, HEREFORDSHIRE: a Half-timber Manor-house of the late 14th Century
(the Gatehouse is 15th Century)

Little is known of the first houses in towns, but judging from the frequent and devastating fires that took place it may be assumed that they were mostly built of wood and thatched with rushes. In Lincoln, however, there may still be seen on Steep Hill two stone houses dating from approximately 1150, one known as the Jew's House. They have been badly mutilated, but some interesting features survive. Both contained originally one room to each storey, the upper ones having fireplaces and being lit by round-headed windows divided into two lights by a central shaft, which can still be seen. From FitzStephen's account of London, it would appear that the two major urban evils at this time were fires and drunkenness. To avoid the former, partition walls of stone between houses were introduced; in FitzAlwyne's Assize it is mentioned that these were of freestone, 3 feet thick and 16 feet high. It is not recorded, however, what measures were introduced to combat the latter evil.

In 1216 Henry III came to the throne, and his long reign, extending over fifty-six years, saw a remarkable increase in the prosperity of the country which is clearly reflected in the development of domestic architecture. Until this period comfort, according to present standards, had been practically unknown; from the thirteenth century onwards came a gradual development of the more civilised side of living. Probably the most important advance in building methods at this time was the evolution of the open-timber roof, whereby it became possible to cover a considerably wider floor area in a single span. This construction, which became highly developed during the following centuries, was a feature unique to English architecture. The roof of St. Mary's Hospital at Chichester is one of the earliest secular examples of it, and dates from the latter part of the thirteenth century.

The king himself led the way in improving the standard of comfort. He possessed eighteen houses scattered about the country, from Southampton to Newcastle-on-Tyne, from Bristol to Rochester; of these, the Tower of London, Westminster and Winchester were perhaps the most important. The Liberate Rolls contain an immense number of instructions for the improvement of these houses, which had been completely primitive up to this time; but by the close of Henry's reign they must have reached a state far in advance of any of those of his subjects. Fireplaces were ordered to be built, windows enlarged and glazed, floors boarded and privies better arranged. Little was said about the strengthening of fortifications. Rooms were usually to be wainscoted in wood, and at Windsor Henry ordered his chamber to be "borded like a ship". Green was the favourite colour for the painting of wainscot or walls, and sometimes figure-pieces were introduced in place of diaper patterns. Edward FitzOtho, keeper of the King's Works at Westminster, was instructed to erect a chimney (i.e. fireplace) in the Queen's Chamber and "on it to cause to be portrayed a figure of winter, which as well by its sad countenance as by other miserable distortions of the body, may be deservedly likened to Winter itself". But decorations usually struck a happier note, and gold stars, roses or, as at Clarendon, "a border of heads of kings and queens" were less harrowing suggestions. The most elaborate decoration was always reserved for the chapels, and there are innumerable orders for the painting of religious figures and "histories" from the Old and New Testaments.

Up to this period, the floor of the hall had consisted merely of beaten earth strewn with rushes, on which the retainers, both male and female, slept. This part of the building came to be known as the "marsh", which suggests that the raised wooden daïs at the end of the room, on which stood the high table, was something of a necessity; and one can speculate on the reason for the order that the door of the hall at Winchester was to be sufficiently enlarged to allow for the entrance of a cart. During the thirteenth century, however, the manufacture of tiles for flooring, which had probably survived precariously in England from the time of the Romans, was considerably developed, and Henry ordered the whole of the hall at Winchester to be paved in this way. The decorative design of tiles, for ecclesiastical use or otherwise, became not one of the least attractive branches of medieval handicraft.

Henry's Liberate Rolls specify for kitchens to be enlarged and new butteries, seweries and larders to be built. Windows were to be glazed with clear glass and made to open, more convenient staircases were to be inserted, while new tables and benches were ordered and, very occasionally, a chair. The instructions for the making of privies were explicit. The usual form was a deep walled pit, which must have been an unsatisfactory arrangement, or, where there was a moat, a drain might descend into it below the surface of the water. . . . At the Tower of London the Constable was ordered to "cause the drain of our private chamber to be made in the fashion of a hollow column". This, presumably, emptied into

15 A HOUSE NEAR LONGDON, WORCESTERSHIRE. A post-and-plaster building of the early 16th Century

16 NAPPA HALL IN WENSLEYDALE, YORKSHIRE: a
15th-Century fortified House of Pele type

the Thames; we can perhaps understand the medieval reluctance to drink water.

The reigns of the first three Edwards cover just over a
hundred years, from 1272 to 1377, during which century ecclesiastical building reached a new stage of Gothic achievement
through the so-called Decorated style to the national Perpendicular. Domestic architecture maintained a corresponding
improvement under the direct inspiration of the gifted
Edward I. His close contact with France, where the standard of
living among the rich was well in advance of that obtaining in
England, enabled him to introduce many amenities into this
country. Its comparatively peaceful state allowed these
civilising ideas to fall on fertile ground, and in the southern
counties at least the advance was rapid. In the North, where
defence remained the first consideration, the improvement
was less marked; towers and bastions were still deemed
essentials where in the south a moat and perhaps a wooden
palisade would have sufficed, as in Yorkshire at Markenfield;
while the pele towers raised as defences for farmers and their
cattle against local mosstroopers or raiders from across the
Border have formed the nucleus of many a later North Country
house, as at Nappa (16) in the same county, and Yanwath
in Westmorland. It may be mentioned here that any gentleman wishing to build a fortified manor-house at this time
had to obtain a licence from the king to "embattle, crenellate
and machicolate", which permission was often widely interpreted, as at Bodiam where, in 1386, Sir Edward Dalyngrigge
took advantage of it to erect an almost impregnable castle.
It was a different matter at Stokesay (1240–1290), which,
despite its Elizabethan additions, remains one of our most
striking and complete examples of a fortified manor-house (13).
Here the same licence was employed by an enriched merchant,
Sir Lawrence de Ludlow, largely to draw attention to his
improved status.

While peace and prosperity made strides under the first
Edward and during the greater part of the reign of the second,
they met with something of a reverse under the third. Although
that king, like his predecessors, displayed a personal interest
in building, as may be seen from the favours he heaped on
William of Wykeham, the state of the country was not such
as to encourage any considerable output of domestic work.
The king's attention was concentrated on wars in France,
while in England thieves, "valiant beggars" and disgruntled
peasants disturbed the peace of civil life. So dangerous indeed

did many parts of the countryside become that there is a record of even the belfry of a church being fortified.

But while it remained prudent to have some protection against robbers, the necessity for defence against neighbours began to disappear. The massive Norman keeps, with their tiny windows and dark rooms, were allowed to fall into decay, while more cheerful habitations with larger windows were built within the protection of moats and curtain walls. There are many examples of this trend, of which the domestic ranges of Carisbrooke Castle are as characteristic as any.

Manor-houses now began to assume the plan that they were destined to retain for three centuries. The hall, open to the roof, with either a central hearth, as at Penshurst, or a wide fireplace in one of the long walls, as at Little Wenham Hall, had an entrance door on either side behind a wooden screen, with a gallery above. To one side of the passage formed by the screen were the service quarters—the kitchen, buttery and other offices. Two openings in the screen led to the hall, which had a daïs raised a foot or so above the floor level across the further end. From this daïs a door opened into a chamber known as the Bower, which was a with-drawing-room for the ladies of the house; above the Bower was the Solar, or sunny room, from the Latin *sol*, used as a bedchamber and reached either by a staircase from the daïs or on the outside.

No house of importance was complete without a chapel, even where the rooms were very few, as at Charney Bassett in Berkshire. At Little Wenham in Suffolk (*circa* 1270), which consisted principally of one large hall with an undercroft, the only room opening from it was given over to a chapel dedicated to St. Petronella; and at Old Soar near Plaxtole in Kent (*circa* 1300), which is even smaller, there is the same arrangement. It must not be supposed, however, that the chapels, any more than the churches, were entirely used for devotion. They were indeed considered convenient places of retirement from the pandemonium of the communal hall; business was transacted there, and any discussion or occupation which required privacy. Churches, similarly, were the general meeting-places of the inhabitants of towns and villages, where barter and exchange took place and sometimes entertainments were given. Not for several centuries did it become customary for conversation in a church to be carried on in whispers.

Often large barns, outhouses and dovecotes were grouped

17 GREAT DIXTER, NORTHIAM, SUSSEX : the Great Hall, with its open-timber Roof (*circa* 1450)

18 GIFFORDS HALL, STOKE-BY-NAYLAND, SUFFOLK: the
Interior of the Great Hall (mid-15th Century)

about the manor-house to form a courtyard, as at South Wingfield and Cothay (19); this was entered through a gate-house and protected by a moat and drawbridge as may still be seen in the arrangement of Stokesay (13). Such windows of the hall as faced outwards remained small and discouraging, but those overlooking the court grew larger and far more elaborate.

As the fourteenth century advanced, it became usual to light the daïs with a long oriel—a practice that was to endure for over 150 years. There is an excellent early example of this at Eltham Palace in Kent, dating from *circa* 1480, while the tall lovely window at Horham Hall in Essex (26) was built some thirty years later. The gloom of the older buildings was a thing of the past.

During the reigns of the Edwards, domestic life also underwent considerable changes. If the hall was still the centre of life in the manor-house, where

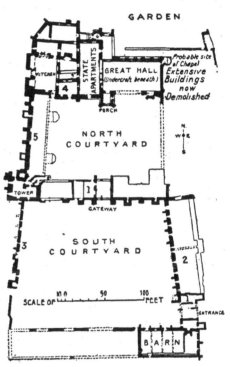

SOUTH WINGFIELD MANOR-HOUSE, DERBYSHIRE (*circa* 1440)

master and servants met for meals and recreation, it was no longer both the sleeping and living-room of most of its inhabitants. The lord and his family now retired to the Bower or Solar for the night, while as the extent of the offices beyond the buttery screen increased, the floor of the hall was used less and less for sleeping, at any rate by the female servants. Its furnishing, however, continued to be of the simplest nature. Tables and benches were the only movables, chairs being practically unknown except for that occupied by the master of the house in the centre of the high table on the daïs (the Coronation Chair at Westminster is an elaborate survival of this type of chair, dating from the thirteenth century). It was at about this time that knives and spoons were first introduced, but their use was by no means general for another century or more, and there is no record of table knives actually being made in England until 1563. Forks achieved an even more belated popularity, and for a long time their use was looked upon as an affectation. Piers Gaveston, characteristically, had "three silver forks for eating pears", and Princess Joan in 1347, less lavishly, "one iron fork". Chaucer, writing in 1388, describes the manner of eating with her fingers of Madame Eglantine, the enterprising prioress, whose French accent was after the school of Stratford-atte-Bow:

> She let no morsel from her lippes fall,
> ne wet her fingers in her sauce deep.
> Well could she carry a morsel, and well keep,
> that no drop ne fell upon her breast.

Her method of drinking was equally graceful, and she can confidently be regarded as a fourteenth-century model of table deportment. But manners were not always so impeccable, and there must have been a real need for the many books of etiquette composed at this time. They are full of useful hints:

> Burnish no bones with your teeth
> For that is unseemly.

> Dip not thy meat in the saltcellar
> But take it with thy knife.

> Pick not thy teeth with thy knife
> Nor with thy finger ends.

And so forth. . . .

As has been seen, Henry III had already ordered the windows of his houses to be glazed. But glass was still rare, and windows were usually shuttered, at least in the lower lights, for which reason these were often divided by transoms, as at Winchester and Stokesay. Sheets of horn and linen dipped in wax were unsatisfactory substitutes for glass, but were largely used. The rare glazed windows were usually removable, so that the fortunate possessors of these luxuries were able to take them down when they left their castle or manor-house and carry them with the rest of the household impedimenta to the next stopping place.

England was far behind the Continent in its use of glass, and there is no word of its manufacture in this country before the fifteenth century, the first definite mention being in the contract for the glazing of the Beauchamp Chapel at Warwick in 1439. The Low Countries were the source of our supply, and from them we imported it in exchange for our staple product of wool, together with barley for the breweries of Ghent and Bruges. Painted windows for churches are mentioned very early, but no records exist of the domestic use of glass until the thirteenth century. It is difficult to account for its tardy popularity, as the cost was not prohibitive, but the fact that it was still sufficiently opaque to coin the fourteenth-century phrase "her eyen grey as glass" may have been one cause.

To Eleanor of Castile, wife of Edward I, must be given the credit for the introduction of carpets, although rushes survived as the most usual floor-covering for many years. Queen Eleanor also used hangings to cover the walls of her rooms, which are rather disparagingly described as "hung like a church", the latter having been previously the only place where such decorations had been seen. The custom of painting walls, which had been general under Henry III, declined gradually, and its place was taken by hangings of tapestry imported from Arras or Paris, and later by tapestry of London manufacture. So popular did this practice become that those who could not afford the genuine stuff hung their walls with a worsted substitute manufactured in Norfolk, or even with canvas painted to simulate tapestry. The tapestry proper was woven over with lively designs: "leopards of gold, falcons, swans with ladies' heads, stars, birds, griffins, eagles and flowers", to mention but a few. Heraldic tapestries were also popular.

When the king or a nobleman travelled he took his hangings with him. Froissart describes how the Duke of Lancaster was able to astonish the Portuguese by hanging his lodgings between Monson and Magassa with the richest tapestry, "as if he had been at one of his manors in England". This form of decoration is portrayed in many medieval manuscripts such as Harl. MSS. 4378–9 and the Luttrell Psalter.

Little is known of the general furnishing of bedrooms. Henry III ordered two benches to serve as beds for himself and his queen, so it may be supposed that even the most sumptuous examples were little more than boards on a support, with a tester covering the head. Thus a comfortable mattress became an important item, and great attention was paid to it, as appears from the fact that the name of Henry III's mattress-maker, William Joyner, has survived. The royal mattresses were covered with silk or other rich stuff and quilted; upon them were laid linen sheets, manufactured in the South-west of England, and a counterpane. A bolster was a usual appendage.

Although the furniture remained primitive, the eating and drinking vessels had reached an advanced stage. The high table was covered with a linen cloth and the platters were of pewter, with squares of wood for the servants, as may still be seen in some college halls; but at the king's table silver, or even gold, plate was used. The use of glass for drinking vessels was rare but not unknown; glass cups were occasionally imported from Venice and were looked upon as precious possessions. Commoner materials were horn and earthenware.

It was quite usual for two or more people to eat off the same platter and drink from the same cup, and it would appear from many references that it was looked on as something of a compliment to share a dish. Hands were scrupulously washed before meals, grace followed, and the minstrels would then begin their music. The latter were a popular feature in the houses of the rich and are often referred to by Froissart and other writers. They were supported by "fools, jesters and mimics", and the result must have been diverting to say the least of it.

Little mention is made by contemporary writers of conditions of life among the peasantry, but these, as can be gathered from the valuable researches of Dr. Coulton and others, were of the most primitive kind. Chaucer describes the narrow cottage of the poor widow:

> Full sooty was her bower and eke her hall
> In which she eat many a slender meal . . .

and even as late as 1610 Bishop Hall inveighs against the still wretched habitations of many of the cottar class:

> Of one bay's breadth, God wot! a silly cote
> Whose thatched sparres are furr'd with sluttish soote
> A whole inch thick, shining like black-moor's brows,
> Through smok that down the head-less barrel blows:

19 COTHAY, WEST SOMERSET : a Manor-house Group of *circa* 1480

20 GREAT CHALFIELD, WILTSHIRE : a Stone Manor-house of *circa* 1480

21 THAME PARK, OXFORDSHIRE : the former Abbot's Lodging

At his bed's-feete feeden his stalled teme;
His swine beneath, his pullen ore the beame:
A starved tenement, such as I gesse
Stands straggling in the wasts of Holdernesse;
Or such as shiver on a Peake-hill side,
When March's lungs beate on their turfe-clad hide.

With the deposition of Richard II in 1399, and his death the following year in Pontefract Castle, the line of the Plantagenet kings came to an end, and the fifteenth century opened upon the disturbed reigns of the houses of York and Lancaster. Not until the third quarter of the century were the troubled waters of English life calmed by the accession of the Tudors.

In a period of war and bitter internal dissension, pervaded by a pessimism that can only be compared with that of our own time or of the age of Catullus, English architecture achieved a gradual florescence that has only of recent years gained the appreciation due to it. True, the masoncraft was often less meticulous, its application more stereotyped, the conception less sternly virile; yet there is no doubt that in the "Perpendicular" that followed upon the brief transient loveliness of "Decorated" can be recognised the first individual expression of the English genius for building, an utterly vernacular style without peer or precedent in other countries. As was natural in an age dominated both in its material and spiritual life by the Church, the domestic output lagged somewhat behind the ecclesiastical. It is true that throughout the reigns of the Edwards immense labour and expense had been lavished on the building of castles, castles destined no less for defence and aggression than to reflect the medieval ideal of Chivalry that found its proudest expression in the circle of Edward III and his sons. This spirit was to endure well into the next century; at Tattershall, for instance, the vast brick keep erected by Lord Cromwell about 1435 belongs to the form of a much earlier date and is in striking contrast to the almost domestic manor-house at South Wingfield built for the same nobleman a few years later.

Though the need for defensive buildings was not quite past, as appears from a study of the Paston Letters which cover the greater part of the fifteenth century, there is no doubt that a far higher standard of comfort was beginning to prevail among a rising class of country gentry, of which the Pastons themselves were typical,—people not ashamed to apprentice a son to a trade, who were gradually superseding by numbers the proud remote nobility of the earlier Middle Ages. Just as to-day we can glimpse the promise of a "brave new world" beyond the span of our present troubles, so the fifteenth-century Englishman was beginning to anticipate, half-unconsciously at first, something of the golden equilibrium of the Tudor culmination, and to seek new preoccupations

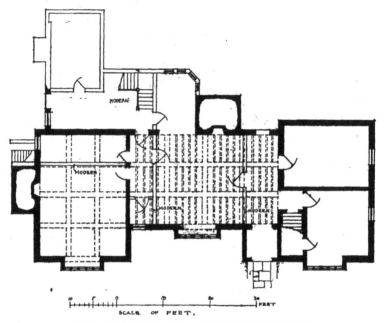

THE LEY, WEOBLEY: A MANOR-HOUSE PLAN
OF THE SIXTEENTH CENTURY

among the arts of peace. The house was now no longer conceived as an amorphous group of rooms; some symmetry was introduced into the planning, the central hall being usually flanked by two roughly balanced projecting wings, as at Cothay in Somerset (*circa* 1480) (19), Great Chalfield in Wiltshire (*circa* 1480) (20), and Ockwells in Berkshire (*circa* 1465). Whether built of stone as the first two, or of timber and brick as the last, it was an arrangement that continued in favour until well into the sixteenth century, and can still be clearly distinguished in many sturdy yeomen's houses in Kent and Sussex.

A very important innovation of the fifteenth century was

22   OXBURGH HALL, NORFOLK: the multi-storeyed Gatehouse
of *circa* 1482

23   SUTTON PLACE, SURREY: the Courtyard Façade of the early
16th Century, built of brick with Terra-cotta enrichments

24 MERE HALL, NEAR DROITWICH, WORCESTERSHIRE: the
rich West-Midland Half-timber of the later 16th Century

the revival of building in brick. Tile-making, as has been seen, had been encouraged during the previous century, but the use of brick remained rare, and Little Wenham Hall in Suffolk, which dates from the later thirteenth century, stands as a lonely example of its employment in a domestic building at that period. Nevertheless it had long been in use in France, and it is possible that it was from their campaigning across the Channel during the Hundred Years' War that English gentlemen acquired their first taste for it. At first colonies of Flemings were imported to make the bricks; it is reported that Sir Roger de Fienes brought over a small army of brick-makers in 1440 to prepare for the erection of his castle at Hurstmonceux, which was one of the earliest large buildings to be completed in the revived material.

While the usual medium for important buildings remained stone, supplemented by flint and rubble in districts without accessible supply, as increased accommodation was required rooms were often added in *pisé*, or post and plaster, in a fairly haphazard manner, and attached to the main structures by pent-roofed passages of the same materials. Henry III ordered an apartment with a lean-to roof and a plaster chimney to be built against the wall of a tower at Windsor for the accommodation of the Bishop of Laodicea, and this was typical of many structures raised for a temporary emergency and later, perhaps, allowed to fall into decay. The majority of smaller manor-houses, of which Eastington Hall in Worcestershire (15), dating from the late fifteenth century, is charmingly typical, were built of the same rather flimsy materials—little more than a timber framework filled in with plaster of wattle and daub. Such buildings have exhibited astonishing powers of resistance, but examples from the earliest period are rare, Lower Brockhampton in Hereford-shire (14), which dates partly from the fourteenth century, being perhaps the most notable.

Windows now became larger and more elaborate, and oriels were no longer exclusively confined to the hall but often overlooked an inner courtyard from an upper floor. External decoration became richer, depending largely for its effect on the graceful cusped stone panelling of Perpendicular practice, and in half-timber buildings the carving of barge-boards and corner-posts was often of great elaboration, as at Ockwells in Berkshire and Mere Hall in Worcestershire (24). Gables were surmounted by finials, often conventionally carved in the form of animals with reference to the arms of

E

the owner of the house. Heraldic weather vanes in metal, as at Oxburgh Hall in Norfolk (15), were another popular feature.

The general arrangement of the house, however, showed little change. In larger examples such as Haddon, where there are two courts, the hall was placed for security between them, though at South Wingfield Manor it is placed on the far side of the inner quadrangle, the precipitous fall of the ground beyond it being considered sufficient protection. Another development of the new spirit of the century was the dawn of a desire for more privacy, which often led to a considerable increase in the number of rooms. The master's end of the building was no longer confined to a Bower and Solar, but was enlarged by the addition of bedrooms. More attention was paid to kitchens, which were now no longer haphazard erections of timber but strongly built as structural units of the houses. Other offices were improved in the same way; privies were increased in numbers, but do not seem to have been bettered in design.

There are many instances of the larger rooms of houses built during the fourteenth and fifteenth centuries being divided up to improve the accommodation without further structural addition. Stoneacre in Kent, for instance, is a timbered house dating from 1480 with a large central hall and two rooms at each end on two floors; fifty years later a beamed ceiling was inserted in the hall dividing it in half, two rooms being formed above, and partitions erected in the Solar to make still further bedrooms. More attention was also paid to convenience. At Hurstmonceux the plans show an ingenuity far in advance of the time; galleries and corridors gave free access to most rooms, and the chamber of the lady was so placed that through a small window she could keep a watchful eye on the servants in the kitchen.

Tapestry and hangings continued to increase in popularity, and from illustrations in Harleian MS. 2278 of a bedroom of the reign of Henry VI it can be seen that the beds were freely hung with tapestry, but that the windows remained uncurtained. In the will of Joan, Lady Bergavenny, dated 1434, there is a detailed list of bed furniture: "a bed of yellow swans, with tapetter of green tapestry with branches and flowers of divers colours, and two pairs of sheets of Raynes [Rennes], a pair of fustian, six pairs of other sheets, six pairs of blankets, six mattresses, six pillows . . . and one pane of minever". Bedding was clearly one of the most important of household items.

26 HORHAM HALL, ESSEX (*circa* 1510) : the East Front, showing the Oriel to the Great Hall

27 COMPTON WYNYATES, WARWICKSHIRE : the West and South Sides, with the " Best Garden " laid out in 1895. The House dates from various periods from 1450 to 1523

But in spite of these improvements knowledge of hygiene lagged far behind. Even as late as the end of the fifteenth century Erasmus, writing after a first visit to England, presents a picture that is far from pretty. "The floors are commonly of clay, strewed with rushes, so renewed that the substratum may be unmolested for twenty years, with an ancient collection of beer, grease, fragments, bones, spittle and everything that is nasty." To this deplorable state of the floors, and to the general lack of ventilation, he attributes the frequent plagues that visited England.

The Normans had introduced the custom of two meals a day, and until the fifteenth century this had remained the practice among the upper classes. Now four became more general: a substantial breakfast at about seven, dinner at ten, supper at four, and "liveries", a heavy culminating meal between eight and nine, eaten in bed. (In a dark world it was still a matter of "early to bed and early to rise".) Dinner was the chief function of the day and was eaten in the hall, master and retainers sitting down together, the former with his family and friends at the high table, the latter below the salt. As early as the close of the fourteenth century, however, the rich occasionally sat apart from their retainers and ceased to preside in hall even at the main meal of the day, a tendency severely denounced by the author of *Piers Plowman*:

> Wretched is the hall where the lord and lady will not sit.
> Now have the rich a rule to eat by themselves . . .

Fingers remained the usual instruments of eating. The food itself was more remarkable for quantity than for quality, although the most lavish ingredients were used, one of the few refinements being the introduction of a dish called a "subtlety", which consisted of figures of people or animals fashioned in jelly, often with some punning label attached to exercise the possibly fuddled wits of the guests.

The installation feast of George Neville to the archbishopric of York has been fully recorded. It consisted of a hundred and four oxen and six wild bulls, a thousand sheep, three hundred and four calves, as many swine, two thousand pigs, five hundred stags, bucks and roes, two hundred and four kids, twenty-two thousand five hundred and twelve fowl, twelve porpoises and seals, and, in addition, fish, pastries, tarts, custards and jellies, and three hundred quarters of wheat. The drink consisted of three tons of ale, a hundred

tons of wine and a pipe of hippocras. It is not recorded, however, how many sat down to this more than ample repast.

The fare of the poor, one fears, was of a less substantial
nature, and during the civil wars thousands died of star-
vation; but it is consoling to read in Fortescue, who wrote
towards the end of the fifteenth century, that "the commons
of England never vouchsafed to drink water except for a
penance".

With the death of Richard III on Bosworth Field in 1485,
and the accession of Henry VII, the Wars of the Roses
reached their end, and the prosperous era of the Tudors
began. The Middle Ages were past.

Ecclesiastical architecture, which had reached its zenith of
Gothic achievement during the fifteenth century, was already,
perhaps, on the downward grade when it was dealt its *coup
de grâce* by Henry VIII's violent measures against the monasteries—measures which, however fatal to church architecture,
gave, by the spread of wealth they entailed, an immense
impetus to the building of great houses. The Peasant Revolt
had been the first organised attack on the Feudal System;
the Wars of the Roses hastened its lingering death. The old
landlord families were now for the most part ruined or exter-
minated, and the new "backbone of England" was quietly
consolidating its position. Never before or since in the history
of this country has there been so sudden a rise of the newly
enriched, such a surge of new families to power and pro-
minence either through commerce or the favours of the king.
At this period many of the great names of England are heard
for the first time: Cavendish, Cecil, Russell, Thynne, Herbert.

The principal criterion of achieved position was the possession of a great house with sufficient accommodation for the
entertainment of the king and his retinue. Fortified castles,
so far from the spirit of the times, were, in many cases, left
to decay, while private palaces, so vast as to be rarely exceeded
in size even by the follies of the eighteenth and nineteenth
centuries, arose in all the southern parts of the country.
This wave of enthusiasm for building seems to have swept
all grades of the community from king to yeoman; even
Henry VII, most parsimonious of princes, erected a new
palace at Sheen on the site of a former building destroyed
by fire. It was of interest as being the first royal residence to
be built in England on a single corporate plan. Pictures of
it survive, together with a minute description of the interior.

28 SANDFORD ORCAS MANOR-HOUSE, DORSET, BY ITS CHURCH. A delightful group of the early 16th Century

29 BRYMPTON D'EVERECY, SOMERSET: the Entrance Front (early 16th Century). The Porch is an addition in Georgian Gothic

30 GIFFORDS HALL, WICKHAMBROOK, SUFFOLK: the Solar (mid-16th Century)

31 OAKWELL HALL, NEAR BIRSTALL, YORKSHIRE:
a Northern stone Manor-house of the early 16th Century

32 MIDDLE LITTLETON, GLOUCESTERSHIRE: a Typical
Cotswold Manor-house of the 16th Century, now a Farm

33 HENGRAVE HALL, SUFFOLK (*circa* 1525-38): the rich Entrance Front

The principal external features were the several large-windowed towers surmounted by ogee-shaped cupolas; tall chimney-shafts shot up amongst a forest of turrets. The hall was 100 feet long and 40 feet wide, the "privy lodgings" comprised 36 rooms, and an open corridor with a gallery above, 200 feet long, adjoined the garden. The greater part of the structure was of stone, but the chimneys were of brick, the cupolas being lead-covered. Taken as a whole, the building was the prototype of a style which was to be freely employed for great houses during the century that followed, a style of which Hengrave Hall in Suffolk is, perhaps, the finest extant example.

The great body of houses that arose at this period, however, was of less ambitious design. Built completely of stone, or of brick with stone quoins and stone-mullioned windows, there was still a small show of defence in battlemented parapets and tall entrance towers—a gesture of bravado given the lie by the larger and more elaborate windows. At Thame Park in Oxfordshire (21), which dates from very early in the sixteenth century, there are several very domestic little bows, and at Sutton Place in Surrey, built on more majestic lines a few years later, the main windows, each of which is divided into six lights by shafts and transoms, are very large (23). Houses of any size were still built around a central courtyard which was entered through a towered gateway, the latter generally incorporating a large central oriel, as at Hampton Court and Cowdray. The ranges were seldom more than one room thick, leading one into another around all four sides of the court. The principal windows gave inwards upon the court, and the boldly projecting chimney-stacks were often built against the outside walls, as in the west wing of Gainsborough Old Hall in Lincolnshire, where their regular succession forms a distinct feature of the design. At first the stacks were simply stepped as they ascended, and were topped by some simple shaft in stone or brick. Soon brick chimneys were found to lend themselves to intensive decoration, and during the reign of Henry VIII reached a fantastic pitch of elaboration. Twisted and counter-twisted, diapered, panelled and surrounded by bands of ornament, no decoration was too minute for the expert craftsmen of the period. Some of the most striking examples are to be seen in the Eastern Counties in such houses as St. Osyth's Priory in Essex and Thurston Hall near Hawkedon in Suffolk. But with the coming of Italian detail, these displays of national ingenuity were restricted, and the early Elizabethan chimney is a less fantastic and vivacious affair.

The popularity of brick as a building medium increased rapidly during the reign of Henry VIII and led to the erection of some of the most romantic buildings England has ever seen. Of these, Compton Wynyates in Warwickshire (27) is one of the most famous and certainly one of the most lovely. Although begun soon after 1450, it owes its present appearance to the early years of the following century; and with its walls of rosy brick, timbered gables, oriel windows and happily grouped towers it is indeed an exquisite flower of the Tudor domestic style, so soon to be complicated and debased by the introduction of misplaced and misunderstood classical detail. The first breath of Italian influence can be seen in the great gatehouse of Layer Marney Hall, Essex, raised in 1525. This beautiful structure, with its twin eight-storeyed towers flanking the entrance arch and two wide oriels, is purely Tudor in form, but the terracotta detail of parapet and windows was supplied by Italian workmen. At Sutton Place, which dates from five years later, the same touch of Italian influence can be seen in the terracotta moldings of the Tudor windows (23), and in the symmetrical composition of the elevations to the court.

No more excellent houses have been built in this country than during the middle-Tudor period. No efforts were wasted on unnecessary ostentation, there was no struggle for an unnatural symmetry, and the planning was dictated by the simple requirements of the inhabitants—those jolly hard-headed country gentlemen of the new type whose class was to achieve such distinction under Elizabeth's rule. The national genius for building has seldom shown itself in a happier and less self-conscious mood. Here was an English vernacular indeed.

Henry VIII was an enthusiastic builder, and erected or renovated no less than ten royal residences, Hampton Court being the only one which survives in a comparatively un-altered state. Some of the royal activity may have been prompted by feelings of rivalry with his fellow monarchs, Francis I of France and Charles V of Spain, who were them-selves embarking on schemes on a scale not yet contemplated in this country. Henry made every effort to lure over artists from the Continent, but both Raphael and Titian, to whom he made the most munificent overtures, declined to leave

34 KENTWELL HALL, SUFFOLK: the Entrance Front and
Moat (mid-16th Century)

35 MORETON OLD HALL, CHESHIRE : the Entrance Front (mid-16th Century), from beyond the Moat. The Top Floor, which contains the Long Gallery, is said to have been added later in the same Century

Italy. Torrigiano, however, was persuaded to come in 1516 to design the tomb of Henry VII at Westminster, and Hans Holbein, during his many years in England, turned his attention to most forms of decorative art. Of his architecture, however, little survives except a summer-house at Wilton, originally the porch of the old house said to have been built from his designs (117).

Towards the middle of the sixteenth century much decorative detail that was the shopwork product of foreign craftsmen working in this country began to be employed in domestic building; an example of this trend is the entrance front of Hampton Court Palace, which incorporates terracotta roundels containing heads of the Roman emperors and an elaborate cartouche of Wolsey's coat-of-arms in the same material. At Nonsuch Palace near Cheam, built for his own use by Henry VIII, there was no vacant space of wall without its decoration, no gable without its pinnacle, no turret without its cluster of weather-vanes. But this frenzied elaboration was no more than the trappings upon the sober forms of Tudor Gothic, and it was not until much later in the century, when architects as well as craftsmen began to be imported from abroad, that any radical change in structure or planning became apparent.

The H- and E-shaped houses remained popular throughout the sixteenth century. It would seem unlikely that they were ever thus built out of compliment to the Tudor sovereigns, as these plans were almost the only known alternatives to the "hollow square", which remained equally popular. Were it recorded that houses had ever been built on the more complex plan of an M the theory might be more easily substantiated. John Thorpe, it is true, designed a house in the form of his own initials, I.T., and wrote beneath the plan:

These two letters I and T,
Joyned together as you see,
Is meant for a dwelling house for me.
Iohn Thorpe.

But this fantasy, so very much in the Elizabethan manner, was never carried out . . .

As the sixteenth century advanced, it became usual to plan the main reception rooms on the first floor following the Italian convention of a *piano nobile*. This system had been adopted as early as 1441 at South Wingfield Manor, where the great state apartment was raised well above the level of the hall, though in this case it can be regarded as little more than a glorified solar. The inevitable consequence of this enhanced importance of the first floor was that more attention was paid to the staircase. Up to this period a modest stone flight, straight or circular, had been considered sufficient, and the English builders were slow to adopt a more imposing scheme. The great winding stone staircases of France, which date from the early part of the sixteenth century, never had their parallel in this country; indeed, the first half of the century was over before even the broad wooden flights which gave a fairly dignified approach to the state rooms became at all common. It was not until the beginning of the seventeenth century that the staircase came to be considered as an important structural feature of the house. At Knole in Kent, for instance, the example built in 1605 is an elaborate and graceful piece of Jacobean design, but it is modest in comparison with the scale of the building and the number and grandeur of the rooms, to which it gives access; but at Hatfield in Hertfordshire, designed by Robert Lyminge only some five years later, the staircase is given proportionate emphasis both in scale and richness of detail. Gradually, however, architects veered to the opposite extreme, and immense spaces were devoted to grandiose staircases which, in the majority of cases, led only to bedrooms, as the reception rooms by now were generally once again relegated to the ground floor. Astonbury in Hertfordshire is an extreme instance, where two large staircases of excellent Jacobean design are placed in large twin projections at the back of the house, both giving access to a long gallery at the top.

Throughout the Tudor period the principal rooms were invariably panelled. The wainscoting of the fourteenth and early fifteenth centuries which consisted of series of narrow overlapping planks fixed vertically around the walls, was now replaced, particularly in screens and partitions, by boards set between upright posts, thus forming recessed panels. These panels were increasingly carved with the familiar "linenfold" motive, which, by the beginning of the sixteenth century, had reached the highest pitch of elaboration. Good examples of the earlier linenfold can be seen at Paycocks in Essex, and of the later in the splendid long gallery of The Vyne in Hampshire (52), which is lined from floor to ceiling with panelling of this type. With the coming of the Renaissance the compartments were usually divided by pilasters, and various motives were introduced, mostly from

36   LITTLECOTE, WILTSHIRE : the Entrance Front (*circa* 1550)

37 DANNY PARK, SUSSEX (mid-16th Century) : the East Front. The Tower rising behind is a recent addition

Flemish pattern-books, such as arcading (79). The restrained
simplicity of the earlier work was replaced by a riot of unnecessary detail.

Fireplaces became much more common during the sixteenth
century, even for smaller rooms. A depressed "four-centred"
arch, carved out of a single piece of stone, was fitted flush
with the wall, the chimney-stack, which projected on the
outside wall, taking the depth of the hearth. The opening
was generally surrounded by appropriate panelling, without,
however, additional ornamental emphasis of any form. Fireplaces of this plain type may be seen at Thame Park and in
Cardinal Wolsey's closet at Hampton Court, both of which
date from *circa* 1525. Early in the reign of Elizabeth the
chimneypiece came to be considered the dominant feature of
a room, surmounted by a richly carved overmantel of heraldic
or "strapwork" design, forming a single unit with the fireplace. Timber ceilings were flat but still constructional. Heavy
chamfered beams stretched from wall to wall supporting the
joists, as in the example at Moreton Old Hall in Cheshire
dating from the mid-sixteenth century, the massiveness of
which comes as something of a surprise after the apparent
fragility of the exterior.

Although the Tudor tradition of building was gradually
to be effaced in most of the great houses built from the spoils
of the monasteries, it continued as a pure stream, untouched
by time and fashion, in manor-houses and cottages scattered
about the countryside. Even as late as the mid-seventeenth
century buildings can be found, such as the stone wing of
Hall-i'-the-Wood near Bolton, in which the early Elizabethan
method lingers little touched by classical detail—while the
post-and-plaster wing, built as early as 1583, differs little,
except in the size of the windows, from such a house as
Moreton Old Hall in Cheshire (35), which dates from half a
century later.

The timbered house, one of the most beautiful products
of English domestic architecture, died hard in Cheshire and
Lancashire, Sussex and East Anglia, districts in which this
form of building was particularly popular and appropriate;
and a number of examples can be found dating from well
into the seventeenth century. The most exuberant specimens
are to be found in the northern counties, where it reached a
pitch of elaboration never attempted in the more sober South
or East. But for beauty of design and excellence of craftsmanship it would be hard to surpass such a house as Paycocks

F

at Coggeshall in Essex (38), which is built on quite a modest scale in the village street and dates from the opening years of the sixteenth century.

At the same time, the stone districts were producing the reserved houses and cottages which may be epitomised as the Cotswold style, and are so admirably suited to the downland country in which they appear. In these remote parts of the country, where building traditions were strong and died hard, a simple variant of Gothic flourished well into the seventeenth century. Ten years after Inigo Jones had completed his Banqueting House at Whitehall in 1622, the men of Sussex were making additions to such a house as Batemans near Burwash in a style that might have been employed by their fathers or even by their grandfathers; and many of the simple manor-houses and cottages that decorate such towns and villages of Gloucestershire as Bibury, Cirencester and Burford might well have been built at any moment during the fifteenth or sixteenth centuries; it is only by the occasional detail of a chimney or a doorway that the march of progress can be detected. The medieval plan was abandoned with even more reluctance than the medieval detail, and the traditional arrangement of a hall flanked by chambers and offices can be found in many smaller houses without other trace of Gothic feeling. Gradually, however, the influence of Renaissance fashion began to permeate the most sequestered corners of the countryside. The larger houses were built or altered to conform with modern taste, and their example was slowly followed in rectories and farm-houses. Nevertheless the Gothic style had only properly been dead in England a brief century or so before it found startling resurrection at the hands of Horace Walpole and other *dilettanti* of the eighteenth century.

38 PAYCOCKS, COGGESHALL, ESSEX: rich East-Anglian
Half-timber of *circa* 1500

PAYCOCKS, ESSEX: Interior

40 PETWORTH HOUSE, SUSSEX (late 17th Century): the Southern
Angle of the West Front, showing the decided French influence

CHAPTER III

THE RISE OF THE ARCHITECT

(*Circa* 1550 to 1720)

AMONG the foreign craftsmen lured to these shores by the lavish offers of Henry VIII was one John of Padua. No surname has ever been assigned to him and he would remain a nebulous, almost mythical figure were not two facts known about him. Firstly he was appointed "Deviser of His Majesty's Buildings" by Henry VIII in 1544, and secondly he was a domestic architect in the same sense as we now use the word. Several extant houses have been credited to him, Longleat in Wiltshire, which was begun in 1567, more persistently, if probably no more correctly, than most. Although his actual achievements remain uncertain, he holds the distinction of being the first domestic architect, with the possible exception of Holbein, to practise in England whose name has come down to us.

John of Padua was patronised by the Protector Somerset for whom he designed Old Somerset House, which stood on the site of the present building of that name. A view of it survives among the drawings of John Thorpe, now in the Soane Museum. Its scholarly façade, sparsely furnished with columns and pediments, must have astonished a generation which had previously regarded the decorative riot of Nonsuch as its criterion of taste.

It cannot be said, however, that either Holbein or John of Padua left any lasting mark on English architecture; they founded no school nor created any immediate break in Tudor tradition. The rise of the Renaissance style in England did not follow, as might have been expected, the sixteenth-century influx of Italian craftsmen; it was not, indeed, directly from Italy that we derived our first main impulse towards classicism, but from the Low Countries, with which our commercial and sympathetic ties were already strong. The break from Gothic came slowly, and the Flemish Renaissance style as first rendered in England would have horrified any contemporary Italian architect by its clumsy exuberance and continued confusion with the traditional vernacular. Nevertheless, in little more than half a century the eccentricities of the late-

Elizabethan builders had developed into the pure but intensely individual conceptions of Inigo Jones and Christopher Wren.

The spread of wealth and prosperity that had continued unabated during the reigns of the Tudors reached its culmintion with Elizabeth. No longer was the new affluence confined to the aristocratic classes; from them it percolated through every stratum of society, even the humblest sharing to some degree in the plenty. There was a feeling of Spring in England; new ideas and impulses were wafted like breezes from the Continent, and a new zest for knowledge, particularly in the spheres of art and literature, was making itself manifest. For the first time it became fairly usual for members of the upper classes to have a critical and constructive knowledge of architecture, a knowledge that was to become an essential part of the educated man's equipment for two centuries. This *expertise* in the layman was largely responsible for the appearance of the trained architect in the first instance. With the later and more complete reliance of the layman on the architect in matters of taste, the standard of knowledge inevitably declined. By the mid-nineteenth century, although enthusiasm for building remained disastrously strong, the critical faculty of the public at large had become almost entirely atrophied.

There are many indications of the new desire of Englishmen to increase their knowledge of Continental buildings. As early as 1568 Lord Burleigh, with thoughts of the great house he was soon to build near Stamford, wrote to Elizabeth's ambassador in Paris asking him to procure one of Philibert de L'Orme's *cahiers*, and in 1611, Robert Peake of Holborn issued as a fine black-letter folio *The First Book of Architecture* "made by Sebastian Serly, translated out of Italian into Dutch and out of Dutch into English". Incidentally, the "translations" of the book were somewhat analogous to those of the Renaissance style as it found its first expression in England. Serly, or Serlio, was a native of Bologna, and produced this large work in five volumes between 1537 and 1547. He had drunk at the fountain-head of Vitruvius and made meticulous measurements of ancient buildings, and his books were a mine of information and inspiration for the English builders, who must have made liberal if inaccurate use of his detailed drawings, although no actual instances can be traced.

Another author who did much to bring the classical style to the notice of the English public was Sir Henry Wotton, traveller, diplomat and scholar (1568–1639). Although never more than an "amateur" of building in the best sense, his *Elements of Architecture*, based on a study of the works of Vitruvius, Palladio and Philibert de L'Orme, show not only an enthusiastic appreciation of the classical style but a practical understanding of the essentials of domestic building far in advance of his age.

He dwells firstly on the care that must be taken in choosing a suitable situation or "posture" for a house. It must not be "subject to any foggy noisomness, from *fens* or *marshes* neer adjoining", "not indigested, for want of *Sun*: not unexercised for want of *wind*". "Malign *Influences*" which give rise to "*Earth-quakes, Contagions, Prodigious births*" should not be entirely disregarded. He finds that "vast and indefinite views" are condemned by good authors. Then a shrewd social, or, as he calls it, "political" hint: do not "build too near a great neighbour as it will mean living on Earth, as *Mercury* is in the Heavens . . . ever in obscurity under brighter beams than his own". He ends this subject by urging that builders should be as circumspect as wooers, and let it never be said of one's house as it was of Mytelene, "a town, in truth, finely built, but foolishly planted".

Then for planning. He compares a house to the human body and comes to the conclusion that the same principles apply to both in that "the Plan of every part is to be determined by the Use"—which, no doubt, was a new idea in Elizabethan building. On the question of aspect he seems a little arbitrary: "the principal chambers of delight, all Studies and Libraries, be towards the east: for the Morning is a Friend to the Muses. All offices that require heat, as Kitchens, Stillatories, would be Meriodional. Cellars, pantries . . . to the north. To the same side likewise all that are appointed to gentle motion, as Galleries." He notes that suitable aspects vary in different countries and realises that "a good *Parlour* in *Ægypt*, would perchance make a good *cellar* in *England*".

Next materials. The qualities of various woods are very sensibly discussed and the foibles of some architects in relation to them—how Leon Battista Alberti insists on all the timber in a house being cut from the same forest, all the stone from the same quarry; while Philibert de L'Orme recommends that the "Lyme" or mortar should be made out of the same stone as the rest of the building. There follow some practical hints on the making of bricks. Occasionally he makes mistakes. In dealing with pillars he denounces the practice of making them swell in the middle, "as if they were sick of some Tympany, or Dropsie", although he owns that even the great master Vitruvius advises it. With staircases he is on safer ground when he suggests that "they should have a very liberal *light*, against all Casualty of *Slips*, and *Falls*"; "that to avoid *Encounters*, and besides to gratify the beholder, the whole *staircase* have no nigard *Latitude*"; and that the steps should never be more than half a foot in height "for our *Leggs* do labour more in *Elevation* than in *Distention*". Then "Touching *Conducts* for the *Suillage*", which he recognises "for the health of the inhabitants, are as considerable, and perhaps more than the rest", he suggests that where there is no running water drains should be relegated to the "most remote, and lowest, and thickest part of the *foundation*, with secret vents passing up through the walls like a *tunnel*, to the wilde Air aloft". This is one of the many ideas he obtained from contemporary Italian usage.

He was strongly averse to the Italian system of placing the doors of reception rooms opposite one another, so that when all were open a long vista was obtained, as it "doth put an intolerable servitude upon all chambers save the inmost". But his disapproval was in vain, for this arrangement was almost universally employed in the great English houses of the following centuries.

It does not appear, however, that Wotton was ever enabled to put his unusual knowledge and sound sense at the service of any building. But that such a book should have been written and probably fairly widely circulated shows the expanding appeal of the technicalities of architecture at this time. Dr. Andrew Borde's famous advice on site and disposition of rooms affords a parallel instance.

Another contemporary publication was *The Metamorphoses of Ajax*; "a Claocinean Satire", compiled by Sir John Harington, Elizabeth's wayward but disarming godson, in 1594. In it the author describes in detail a water closet which he had designed and erected at his house at Kelston near Bath, which was afterwards copied at the Queen's Palace at Richmond. The invention comprised all the essentials of the system employed to-day, but its hygienic principles held no attractions for the Elizabethans and the innovation was soon forgotten, not to be resurrected for more than two centuries.

The names of specific architects were coming to be attached to new houses, but how far their functions embraced the conception and realisation of the completed plan remains

41 BURTON AGNES, YORKSHIRE: the Entrance Front, built between 1589 and 1603

42 WOLLATON HALL, NEAR NOTTINGHAM (to whose Corporation it now belongs).
This vast ostentatious pile was begun in 1580

uncertain. Robert Lyminge, for example, is generally credited
with the design and construction of Hatfield House for the
Earl of Salisbury, which was begun about 1607 and completed
four years later; but from the Hatfield papers it would appear
that several other master-craftsmen were employed, equal if
not superior in status to Lyminge. The charge of the works
was in the hands of Thomas Wilson, who was general super-
visor and paymaster. He was assisted by Simon Basil (Surveyor
of the Royal Works prior to Inigo Jones), and together they
shared the responsibility for seeing that the work was kept
within the estimate of £8,500. This originally had been drawn
up by Lyminge, who in a letter mentions that he is making
an elevation for the gallery; but nowhere does he claim the
authorship of the complete design. His exact connection with
Blickling Hall in Norfolk is similarly uncertain, though in
the church register of that parish he is boldly described as
"the architect and builder of Blickling Hall". Similarly,
Robert Smithson is described in his epitaph in the parish
church as "architect and surveyor unto the most worthy
House of Wollaton".

As has been seen, the office of architect was in some degree
a foreign importation; yet it should be realised that the gulf
between the medieval *custos operi* at the dawn of the sixteenth
century and the Renaissance designer-architect at the close
of the seventeenth was not such a wide one. As the Middle
Ages drew to their close, and the contract system, by which
a builder bound himself to execute a given job within a given
time and for a given sum, often supplying labour, cartage
and materials, arose in its completeness, the working master
was gradually superseded by the independent contractor, who
would appoint a *custos operi*, or surveyor, to supervise the
whole work in its various grades—masonry, carpentry,
smithery and the rest. Both Lyminge and Smithson probably
belonged to this class of surveyors, soon to be dignified by
the name of architects. But the function of the contracting
master-mason continued for long essentially the same, and
there is no vast difference between the fourteenth-century
Henry Yevele, the builder of the Westminster nave, and such
men as Strong and the Kempsters who worked with Wren
at St. Paul's. The latter were still perfectly capable of furnishing a sound design if required, and records exist of their
doing so.

If the office of architect did not reach its full importance
until the advent of Inigo Jones, some interesting figures

emerge during the early experimental years of the classical
Renaissance. Of these John Thorpe, who practised between
1570 and 1610, is the most outstanding. Almost all the vast
houses built at this active period are traditionally connected
with his name, and the difficulty of deciding which should be
placed to his credit is increased rather than diminished by
the extensive collection of "Thorpe Drawings" preserved at
the Soane Museum. For Thorpe not only collected his own

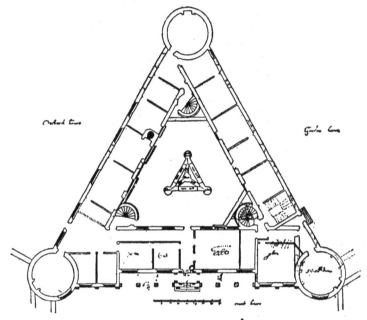

LONGFORD CASTLE: THORPE'S PLAN

designs, but also made drawings from the plans and "up-
rights" of other surveyors. The majority of these, so far
from being working plans, are made from the finished
buildings. In any case they cover such a variety of styles
that it would hardly be possible for them to be the conceptions of a single designer. Burghley House, Kirby Hall (62),
Longford Castle (50) and even Montacute (43), have all in
their time been connected with Thorpe's name, and of Kirby
and Longford there are elevations and plans in the collection
that correspond almost exactly to the houses as built. Longford, which was built for Thomas Gorges between 1578 and
1591, is one of the most fantastic houses ever conceived in

43 MONTACUTE HOUSE, SOMERSET, FROM THE SOUTH-EAST. Built
between 1580 and 1600, this lovely building is now cared for by the National Trust

44 "HARDWICK HALL, MORE GLASS THAN WALL." . . . The
West Front of the great Derbyshire House, completed in 1597

45 HATFIELD HOUSE, HERTFORDSHIRE (begun in 1608): an Air-view from the South, showing the older Hall, the Garden Lay-out, and the proximity of the House to the Village

this country, and exemplifies an architect in his desire to produce something new taking some shocking liberties with the classical style. It was planned in the form of a triangle, with a round battlemented tower at each corner. These were intended as emblematic of the Trinity and are so labelled on the plan; the lines connecting them represent less obvious theological points. But though original to the point of eccentricity in his elevations and planning, Thorpe, if he was indeed the architect, remained faithful to the favourite traditional feature of English domestic architecture, the great hall, which, with its entrance behind the buttery screen and windows looking out through the surprising façade, is moulded into the plan as carefully as it would be into that of the most conventional Elizabethan mansion. At Wollaton (42) which, as has been remarked, is usually ascribed to Smithson, the hall, though placed unconventionally in the very centre of the vast ornate pile of masonry that is the house, remains the principal room and was originally entered in the usual way through a stone screen. Longford (115) was considerably enlarged during the nineteenth century, but happily both these astonishing houses remain sufficiently unaltered to exemplify the extremes of a fortunately transient style.

While Thorpe, the Smithsons, Lyminge and others were scattering vast houses over a shaggy countryside, there was also in the heart of England a rich county landowner who, for his own satisfaction, was designing and erecting buildings on his estate which, though small in scale, have surely never been surpassed for oddity of conception. This talented gentleman was Sir Thomas Tresham of Rushton in Northamptonshire. True his output was small, consisting of no more than three buildings, all of which survive—the Market-house at Rothwell, the Triangular Lodge at Rushton, and the unfinished Lyveden New Buildings near Oundle. Here again the ubiquitous Mr. Thorpe would seem to have had some hand in the planning, for there are alternative schemes for Lyveden in the collection; but the general conception must certainly have been Tresham's.

Born about 1543, Sir Thomas, who was a man of intensely religious feeling, suffered perpetual persecution for recusancy, and, after many fines and imprisonments, was restricted to living on one or other of his estates. There he erected these small but remarkable buildings, in the decoration of two of which he was able to find outlet for his religious fervour so complex as to escape the watchful eye of orthodoxy. The

G

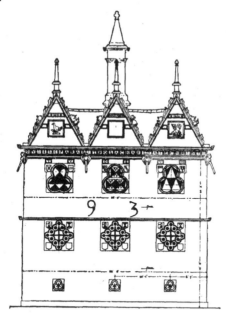

North Elevation.

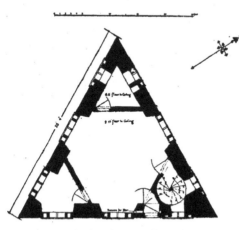

THE TRIANGULAR LODGE, RUSHTON
ELEVATION AND PLAN

Market-house is the simplest, consisting of one great room above an open arcade, the exterior walls covered with a galaxy of heraldic shields. The Triangular Lodge is more elaborate. It is surrounded by friezes of obscure texts, and, wherever possible, the decoration, which is copious and varied, is divided into multiples of three. The main conception of the building, indeed, is based on this pious number; the other numerals carved on the walls still baffle explanation. Lyveden, on the other hand, was built in the shape of an equal-armed cross with a bow-window at the extremity of each arm. It was intended as an occasional residence, and comprises hall, sitting-rooms, kitchen and three bedrooms. It symbolises the Passion, the emblems of which, seven in rotation, are carved on a frieze running round the building above the windows of the main floor. Above the first floor is a second frieze of sentences from the Vulgate, so arranged that the words

46 COTTERSTOCK HALL, NORTHAMPTONSHIRE (early 17th Century). Notice the Flemish influence in the Central Gable

47 ANDERSON MANOR, DORSET (1620): the Entrance Front

48 CANONS ASHBY, NORTHAMPTONSHIRE: the Garden Front, chiefly dating from the early 17th Century

Jesus and *Maria* appear on each side of the terminating bows. Tresham died before it was completed, but after many vicissitudes the shell has been preserved by the National Trust— another example of its intelligent benefaction. These buildings are the most extreme products of an insatiably experimental age, and are perhaps more remarkable as examples of the intellectual curiosity inspired by the new humanism than as works of art— which they certainly are not. Their literary parallel may be found in works of the calibre of Lyly's *Euphues*.

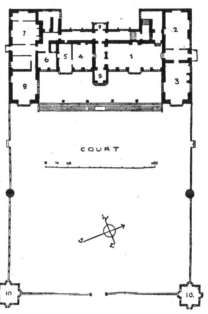

MONTACUTE, SOMERSET, GROUND
PLAN (1580)

1. Hall   2. Drawing-room
3. Large Dining-room
4. Small Dining-room
5. Sitting-room   6. Pantry
7. Kitchen   8. Servants' hall
9. Porch   10. Garden-houses

Beyond the surface exuberance of the new "classicism", the planning and internal arrangement of houses changed slowly. The vast sums now lavished on private building allowed a considerable increase in the number of rooms, with a corresponding magnificence of decoration, but these were generally added to a structural nucleus representing the traditional arrangement. More space was given over to the comfort of guests; at Kirby, for example, the long sides of the courtyard are composed of lodgings, each with a separate door opening upon the court and no further internal communication with the body of the house. Such accommodation was particularly necessary when the entertainment of the Queen was contemplated; her retinue was often so numerous that three or four had to sleep in a room.

Not only were mansions laid out on these vast proportions in order to house the Court; some noblemen went so far as to erect second houses in which to entertain the Queen on her progresses. Thus Lord Burleigh built Theobalds as well as the great house at Stamford, and Sir Christopher Hatton possessed both Holdenby and Kirby. Both these gentlemen would freely admit that they maintained second houses principally for the pleasure of their Mistress.

Meanwhile, designers were realising the advantages of privacy and comfort; more corridors and staircases began to be introduced, and more ingenuity generally to be shown in planning, as at Buckhurst, now unfortunately destroyed, where a real tennis court was incorporated in the plan without undue displacement of the rooms. The interior porch was a makeshift device of this period, of which ornate examples are to be seen at Broughton Castle, Bradninch and Red Lodge, Bristol. With the wider appreciation of classicism, symmetry of elevation became general even in houses which, as Montacute, adhered to the earlier Elizabethan arrangement. But that slavish symmetry of plan advocated and adopted by Palladio was never utterly assimilated in England, even during the later extremes of the national "Palladianism".

One of the principal discoveries of the Early Renaissance architects was that an imposing effect could be obtained by height. For more than a century it had been customary to overawe the approaching visitor with a towering gatehouse, as at Hurstmonceux (*circa* 1450), Oxburgh (1482) (22) and Layer Marney (*circa* 1520); but the principal ranges were seldom more than two storeys high. Now, however, houses would be designed to three lofty storeys, as at Burghley and Hardwick (44), both of which date from about 1580; sometimes they were first raised on a surrounding terrace, as at Wollaton (42). From this platform rose the ornate structure of the house. Starting as a rule rather quietly with ordered rows of large mullioned windows of many lights, framed by pilasters and a cornice (as was achieved so happily in the courtyard of Kirby Hall (*circa* 1572) and less happily at Wollaton), the architect worked up his theme through a decorative crescendo of orders, niches and roundels to a veritable frenzy of invention at the skyline. At Burghley, for instance, which is one of the largest houses built at this time, the body of the design, with its long lines of evenly spaced windows, is majestic and dignified in the extreme, but the eye is distracted by the elaborate and tortured silhouette against the sky. Towers and cupolas, obelisks and coats of arms, a spire, chimneys shaped like columns, nowhere is there

49 WISTON PARK, SUSSEX : an attractive Hybrid, chiefly of the late 16th Century

50 LONGFORD CASTLE, WILTSHIRE: the Entrance Front, by John Thorpe (1580)

51 KNOLE, KENT: the Ballroom (*circa* 1605)

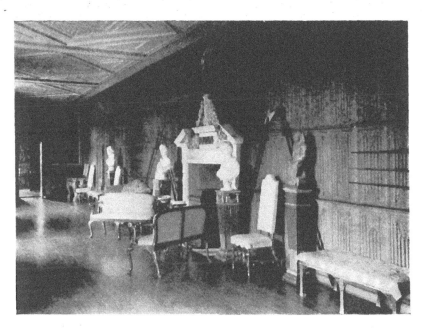

52 THE VYNE, HAMPSHIRE : the Long Gallery (*circa* 1515), with
its splendid array of Linenfold Panelling

53 POWIS CASTLE, MONTGOMERYSHIRE : the Long Gallery
(late 16th Century)

54 KINGSTON HOUSE, BRADFORD-ON-AVON, WILTSHIRE:
a rich symmetrical façade of *circa* 1610

55 KEEVIL MANOR-HOUSE, WILTSHIRE: a quiet design of the
later 16th Century, planned on a Solid Square

rest or peace, or any unity of roof-line to give balance and finish to the composition. Too great enthusiasm and too little discretion were the chief failings of the Early Renaissance builders.

This wealth of clumsy detail and grotesque invention was viewed with considerable disfavour by the *diletantti* of the eighteenth century; Horace Walpole denounced it roundly. "The taste of these mansions", he wrote, "was that bastard style which intervened between Gothic and Grecian architecture; or which, perhaps, was the style that had been invented for the honour of the nobility when they first ventured, on the settlement of the kingdom after the termination of the quarrel between the Roses, to abandon their fortified dungeons and consult convenience and magnificence"—an opinion that might well be held to-day, if the mellowing influence of age did not disarm criticism.

But not only the great were taking advantage of the new domestic security; the lesser gentry, whose numbers have never been larger than during the seventeenth century, were emerging as eagerly as their masters from the gloom of the Middle Ages. The typical manor-house of this period almost invariably conforms to the simple E-shaped plan, though there are occasional examples, such as Keevil Manor in Wiltshire (55) and Whitehall (1578) on the outskirts of Shrewsbury, of medium-sized houses built on an unbroken square. The style remained as faithful to the vernacular as the plan, only borrowing details from the more important structures, though a Renaissance porch became almost invariable. Such a building as Lake House near Amesbury, which dates from late in the sixteenth century, with its reserved chequerwork façade of flint and stone and trim line of gables, owes little to Renaissance influence save in the symmetrical disposition of its features; Montacute (43), designed on a grander scale at the same period, varies from its earlier and humbler prototypes in little save its great height, its elegant finialled parapet and columnar chimneys; while Bramshill in Hampshire, built as late as 1606, has, with its reticent, dignified brick elevations, a much closer affinity with the middle-Tudor period than with the discoveries of Queen Elizabeth's reign.

The cult of height, however, was infectious. Adopted at first only in the vaster mansions, it became towards 1600 a characteristic even of moderate-sized houses built on traditional lines. Burton Agnes in Yorkshire (41), which was begun about 1590, has graceful semi-circular bow windows on the end faces of the short projecting wings that light three lofty floors of rooms, and Chastleton in Oxfordshire, which dates from ten years later, contains, with a semi-basement, no less than five floors. Both these houses were built with a long gallery extending across the entire top floor, but that at Burton Agnes has been divided up. Fountains Hall in Yorkshire, built in 1610 from the materials of the ruined abbey, also rises to five storeys, but in this case the exceptional height is partly accounted for by the slope of the site, which is so steep that at the back only half the house is visible.

During the first decade of Charles I's reign a number of attractive houses were built in what has been called the "Dutch Gable" style. Symmetrically designed, usually on an abbreviated H-plan, and built of brick, sometimes with stone quoins and dressings as at Raynham Hall in Norfolk (*circa* 1630) (67), and generally with wooden mullions, as at Broom Park (1635) in Kent and Swakeleys (1638) in Middlesex, there was invariably a fairly thorough use of classical detail, as at Kew Palace (1631), where the three orders are built up in the centre of the entrance front of the ordinary brick, finely worked by hand. But the gables generally received the most individual treatment—scrolls and whorls, topped by pediments either round or straight, concealed the roof-ends; they could be intensely elaborate, as at Broom, or severely simple, as at Christchurch Mansion in Suffolk. The popularity of this version of the Dutch style, however, was transient, and the seductive gables very soon gave way to the broader pediments of lower pitch of Italian practice. There are a few houses which clearly show the transition from the one style to the other, such as Tyttenhanger and Balls Park, both in Hertfordshire. The former, begun in 1654, is built in the traditional form of a short-armed H, and the pedimented windows, classical in shape, contain the wooden mullions and lead lattices which were so soon to be replaced by sashes. All gables are discarded, and above the third line of windows runs a deep cornice from which springs the simple sweep of roof, on which is set a central octagonal cupola. The building is entirely of brick without any of the usual stone dressings. Balls Park, dating from some years earlier, is a rather simpler composition, the decoration of which is largely confined to pilasters at the corners of the house, plain brick architraves to the windows and a molded brick cornice at the first storey.

Though the planning of houses altered so gradually, and, as has been seen, the hall in its traditional form continued to

56 LILFORD HALL, NORTHAMPTONSHIRE: Dutch Gables and Symmetry in a pleasing Design of 1635

57 GILLING CASTLE, YORKSHIRE (now converted into a School) : the Grand Chamber (*circa* 1575) as it was. A magnificent example of Elizabethan decoration at its best. The stained glass was by Bernard Dininckhoff (1585)

make its appearance behind the most diverse façades, notice-able changes became apparent towards the end of Elizabeth's reign. Examples began to occur of the front door opening boldly into the centre of the hall, which thus lost its old purpose for sitting and eating and became little more than an entrance lobby, a special room being set apart for meals. Aston Hall near Birmingham, which was built during the reign of James I, is an example of this change. At the same time, the long gallery became an inevitable feature even in houses of moderate size, and often occupied nearly half the space of the first floor. Sir Francis Bacon, in his *Essay on Building*, indicates the prevailing conception of a house in the grand manner. One side should be given over exclusively to state purposes, with "only one goodly room" above stairs "for feasts and triumphs". Round an inner court should be stately galleries, "chambers of presence" and bedchambers. These rules were broadly interpreted in the mansions then building about the country for the nobility—Burghley, Hatfield, Knole, Hardwick and, originally largest of all, Audley End.

Inventories of the Elizabethan period throw an interesting light on the trend of furnishing. The principal features were the beds and bedding; of slightly less account were the eating and cooking utensils, while the contents of sitting-rooms consisted of little more than a few tables, an occasional chest and some benches. Here are hitherto unpublished extracts from the Inventory made in 1605 of the contents of the house of a rich Cheshire squire:

> "One standing goyened bed with a tester of greine and yallowe velvett five curtaines of blwe and yallowe saye one feather bedd with a flock bedd under yt a matt a coverlitt foure whyte blancketts a large boulster twoe pillowes with pillowe beires and a whiel bed under the same without eithr bed clothes or furniture.
>
> A standing bed with a tester of blwe & russett five hanging curtaines to the same blewe and yallowe a feather bed a matt and a tick boulster a ladder a coverlitt a chamberpot and a cheire with painted clothes."

Then follow twenty or more other beds in order of pre-cedence which are in striking contrast to the rather prosaic contents of the sitting-parlour:

> "A cheire a paire of Virginlls a little deske towe mappes a little rounde picture a little buffett stoole a paire of andirons a pair of tongues a fier shovell a brasen morter a gridiron

a broken glasse bottell covered with a leather a chafer and a tosting iron.

Limlecke a trumpet a dosse stoole covered with leather a pestell a morter of wood and a cage of wire for a nightingale."

Turning from these spare furnishings of the solar or gallery to the kitchen department, we find:

"Eight pottes and posnetts, a boyler, a brasen morter five dreeping pannes, 3 chafing dishes 2 little pannes, a frying pan, a grid-iron, a sive a brasse pan, a yeiling boole, a skillen 5 Eshnis, 5 cruckes"

and innumerable other pots, pans, basins and tubs. The only comestibles, however, were "xxviii flitches of bacon & a hundred fore score and twee cheeses".

The plate was considerable, and consisted chiefly of silver or "guilt saltes booles & wine ewers". The "Linnene" were mostly "Towells, table clothes" and an immense number of napkins—"damask, with laice worke", or "holland", or "flaxen". Of sheets there were only 10 pairs and one pair of "fustian blancketts".

There is no mention of vessels of glass, though these became increasingly popular and fashionable during the reign of Elizabeth. The fine Italian glass from Murano was still only used by the rich, but the poor had a substitute made of fern and burnt stone. There was no longer any difficulty in glazing windows, and these were expanded to immense proportions, as at Montacute, Astley and Hardwick (44), which latter well deserves the rhyme: "Hardwick Hall more glass than wall". Bacon did not approve of this fashion and objects that "you shall have sometimes faire Houses, so full of Glasse, that one cannot tell, where to become, to be out of the sunne, or cold". He would hardly have appreciated houses in our newest modern style.

While, as has been seen, many foreign craftsmen came to England during the sixteenth and earlier seventeenth centuries, few English "surveyors" or architects improved their knowledge of the trend of Continental taste by study abroad —a fact which, combined with the innate English suspicion of new ideas, accounts for the comparatively slow development of the true classical idea in this country. John Thorpe, it is true, appears to have travelled to some extent, for among his drawings are plans of several French *châteaux*; he also

58   CASTLE ASHBY, NORTHAMPTONSHIRE (early
17th Century): the Great Hall

59 CASTLE ASHBY, NORTHAMPTONSHIRE (early 17th Century) : the View from the Park

studied Du Cerceau's *Les Plus Excellents Bastiments de France* and copied one of the plans, modifying it to suit English conditions. John Shute had been sent by the Duke of Northumberland to Italy in 1550, and had collected his drawings and notes into a book for the profit of others; but he died ten years after his return to England, and no buildings can be attributed to his hand. There was indeed at this period a pronounced pause in the development of the domestic style. Thorpe, Lyminge, the Smithsons had produced their revolutionary buildings, but what was to be the next step? For the past quarter of a century the English Renaissance manner had pleased the rich, the traditional vernacular had sufficed for "middling" people. It required some greater figure to formulate a style that would permeate all classes.

The pause was not for long. Before the first quarter of the seventeenth century had reached its close, Inigo Jones, whose innovations were to have so profound an effect on the course of English architecture for the next century and a half, was producing designs in the purest Palladian manner which were almost at once to attract English taste from the crudities of the late-Elizabethan and Jacobean ages. Born in 1573 of poor parents, he was fortunate enough, while still young, to attract the attention of the Earl of Pembroke, who sent him abroad to study architecture in "Italy and the politer parts of Europe". He returned in 1603, and the next year designed the scenes for Ben Jonson's *Masque of Blackness*, which was presented at Whitehall before the Court. For the years that followed he was employed continuously on stage designing; many of his exquisite drawings for scenery and costumes are preserved at Chatsworth. In 1613 he again travelled to Italy, staying for some time at Vicenza, when he acquired a thorough knowledge of the works of Andrea Palladio (1518-1580), that cold apostle of Vitruvian precept whose conceptions were to form the germ of one of the most productive schools of English domestic building. In 1615 Jones was appointed Surveyor-General of the Works, and four years later started work on the Banqueting House in Whitehall, which was to have formed part of a vast London palace stretching from the riverside to St. James's Park. Three years later he began the Queen's House at Greenwich, not to be completed until 1635.

The last years of the reign of Charles I were too disturbed for much royal, or even humbler, attention to be paid to architecture, and these two superb works remain practically Jones's sole authentic achievements among the many buildings

H

for centuries attributed to his hand. Coleshill in Berkshire (61), long hailed as his masterpiece, is now proved conclusively to have been built by one of his followers, Sir Roger Pratt, while the design of Wilton House (63) and the completed drawings for the proposed Palace of Whitehall are almost undoubtedly the work of his assistant, John Webb. That so much originally credited to him is proved the work of his

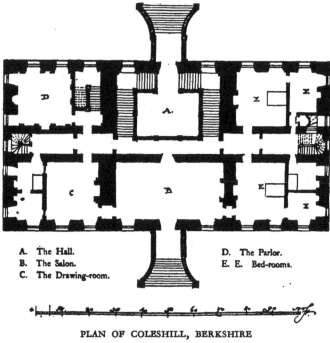

A. The Hall.
B. The Salon.
C. The Drawing-room.

D. The Parlor.
E. E. Bed-rooms.

PLAN OF COLESHILL, BERKSHIRE
BY SIR ROGER PRATT (c. 1650)

school scarcely diminishes his importance. Jones was clearly instrumental in rescuing our domestic architecture from the rut into which it had fallen and in paving the way for the Palladian achievement of the earlier eighteenth century. Finally, he may be regarded as the creator of the office of architect as we know it in England to-day (for better or for worse). He has his Continental parallel in Philibert de L'Orme, who, fifty years earlier, had performed much the same service for France.

The gulf between Renaissance and Gothic building is deep and fundamental. The Gothic house was mainly the product

60 GROOMBRIDGE PLACE, SUSSEX. Wren's name is persistently mentioned
in connection with this delightful house, built at the close of the 17th Century

61 COLESHILL HOUSE, BERKSHIRE. Sir Roger Pratt,
Architect, *circa* 1650

62 KIRBY HALL, NORTHAMPTONSHIRE: the North Front, built between 1638 and 1640 and attributed to Inigo Jones. The ruin of this great house is now cared for by H.M. Office of Works

63 WILTON HOUSE, WILTSHIRE (*circa* 1650) : the South Façade

64 WILTON HOUSE, WILTSHIRE: Detail of the Double Cube Room.
By Inigo Jones and John Webb (*circa* 1650)

of simple contemporary requirements; based on a rough preliminary plan, perhaps scratched on stone by the master-mason, the conception was altered, enlarged or modified as the work progressed, its detail being in the hands of largely independent journeymen, who might add their individual touches of gaiety or gloom. The Renaissance house was entirely the product of one man's mind, and was fully designed, both in plan and elevation, before the work was begun, with the details drawn out "in the large". The proportions were referred to a strict, almost mathematical formula—from which, with characteristic perversity, English architecture was often most happy when it sought to escape. The Early Renaissance builders had endeavoured to combine classical principle with Gothic method, and the results were inevitably surprising.

It was Jones's mission not only to introduce a maturer classicism from Italy, but to be the originator in this country of the developed classical method. His Banqueting House was an innovation of the first importance that set the majesty of an Italian palace before the coldness of a northern sky. As an essay in the Palladian manner is was a timely, vigorous conception of which the façade well interprets the architect's own dictum: "In architecture ye outward ornaments oft (ought) to be sollid, proportionable according to the rulles, masculine and unaffected."

The Queen's House, built for the personal use of Henrietta Maria, is even simpler in design, depending for its effect entirely on the fine proportions of its component parts. Curiously situated bridging the Dover Road, the planning shows as complete a break with tradition as does the façade. The main rooms are all on the first floor following the Italian practice of a *piano nobile*, which is reached by a somewhat restricted circular staircase. There are no passages or corridors, and the rooms lead one from the other. Also persistently attributed to Jones has been the very beautiful north front of Kirby Hall (62) added to the original building by Sir Christopher Hatton about 1638. The arcaded courtyard façade, with its tall pilasters reaching to the cornice, is indeed worthy of the master-hand, but no definite attribution can be made. The same may be said of the staircase and saloon at Forde Abbey in Somerset (76), and the delightful garden-front of Brympton d'Everecy in Somerset (65), which, with its double line of windows surmounted by alternate round and straight pediments, is curiously reminiscent of Whitehall.

Jones was followed by a band of pupils and imitators of whom John Webb (1611–72), his nephew by marriage and assistant from the age of seventeen, was the most prolific. His most considerable work was the rebuilding of the south front of Wilton House, to which he added, with the co-operation of Jones, a group of the most splendid rooms that England has ever seen. The Double and Single Cube Rooms and the Colonnade Room sounded a new note in palatial decoration. The Double Cube Room is 60 feet long and 30 feet high and wide (64); the Single an exact cube of 30 feet. In both the effect of height is diminished by the use of a large cove which springs from a cornice some nine feet below the ceiling. The walls are designed to take the full-length portraits by Vandyke which are framed in panels, with long swags of flowers and fruit pendant between them. The external façade is simple and austere to say the least of it (63), the only ornament being the sculptured figures over the central Vene-tian window and the scroll finish to the windows on the wings.

Thorpe Hall in Northamptonshire, which dates from about 1656, is also generally acredited to Webb. A square building of three storeys, with a hipped roof projecting from a wide cornice, it is intensely Italian in feeling; only in the plan can there be traced a curious reversion to medieval practice. Another house attributed to Webb is Ashdown, which rises like a tower above the Berkshire Downs. Consisting of three storeys above a basement and surmounted by a hipped roof and cupola, it inevitably recalls its neighbour Coleshill with which it is practically contemporary, though the general effect is perhaps less happy.

Hugh May (1622–84) was another of Jones's followers whose best known work, Eltham Lodge in Kent, was com-pleted in 1664. The simple brick elevations, varied on the entrance front by pilasters supporting a flat pediment, produce a pleasant effect of domesticity which is supported by the sane planning of the interior. A somewhat similar house, also built of brick but with stone dressings, is Ramsbury Manor in Wiltshire, which dates from fifteen years later, and, like the great house at Hamstead Marshall in Berkshire, now destroyed, is said to be from the hand of Captain Wynne. Coleshill (61), which was built in 1650, remains the only unaltered example of the genius of Pratt, though Clarendon House in Piccadilly, which survived for only a quarter of a century, was hailed as his masterpiece at the time.

The appearance of this crop of moderate-sized houses of

65 BRYMPTON D'EVERECY, SOMERSET: the Garden Front (late 17th Century). The Design bears a curious family likeness to 'ones' Banqueting House in Whitehall

66 LODGE PARK, NEAR NORTHLEACH, GLOUCESTERSHIRE. Built *circa* 1655 as a
Hunting-box for Sherborne Park (*see front end-paper*)

a revolutionary type (mostly situated, by an odd coincidence, upon the Western chalk) is evidence enough of a change of taste permeating even the most conservative elements of the squirearchy. By the death of Inigo Jones in 1652 domestic architecture seemed settled on the attractive path of Palladianism; but this consummation was not effected so easily. The trend of taste is only radically diverted by some commanding influence, and this, shortly after the Restoration, made an emphatic appearance in the person of Sir Christopher Wren who, far from developing a blind obedience to Palladian precept, formulated a manner most distinctly his own which might well have bound together the many loose strands of English fashion at this time into a second vernacular as appropriate and delightful as that which had flourished with the Tudors. . . . But this was not to be.

Wren was born in 1632, and his first achievements were entirely scholastic. At twenty-one he was Master of Arts and Fellow of All Souls, at twenty-five Professor of Astronomy at Gresham College, at twenty-eight Savilian Professor of Astronomy at Oxford. His earliest interest in building was confined to construction: Inventions for *Better Making and Fortifying Havens, New Designs, tending to Strength, Convenience and Beauty in Building, To Pierce a Rock in Mining,* and so forth. In 1665, however, he travelled to Paris and made a thorough study of the buildings of that city. "I busied myself in surveying the most esteemed Fabricks of Paris and the country round", he wrote—and, later, "I shall bring you almost all *France* on paper". He greatly admired Bernini's design for the Louvre (which was never carried out) and wrote: "The Design I would have given my skin for; but the old reserved Italian gave me but a few minutes' view."

Wren's chance came with the destruction of the greater part of London by Fire in 1666. In that year he was appointed "Surveyor-General and principal Architect for rebuilding *the whole City*; the Cathedral Church of St. Paul; all the parochial Churches (in number fifty-one) and for the disposition of the streets"—office enough, one would think, for a young man of thirty-four. This vast programme he attacked with the vision and vigour that never seemed to desert him during his long lifetime (he died in 1723 at the age of ninety-one). The record of his achievements covers almost every branch of architectural practice from the ecclesiastical splendour of St. Paul's to the secular luxury of Hampton Court. Only in purely domestic work is there something of a gap—and it is by a perverse chance that it was in this field that his influence endured longest. Country gentlemen were on the whole too impoverished and disturbed by the successive events of the Civil War, Commonwealth, Restoration and "Great Revolution" of 1688 to give much thought to building, and Wren's great project for the reconstruction of London on a consistent plan was defeated by conservative prejudice. England was robbed of what might have been one of the most majestic cities in Europe; nevertheless, even to-day there is hardly a country town without its comfortable-looking house in the Wren tradition, hardly a stretch of country without its pleasant "Wrenish" manor-house.

No style could be better adapted to moderate needs. These intelligently planned houses, with their simple brick façades and well-spaced windows allowing ample light and air, seem to reflect the most reasonable traditions of English living, and it is hardly surprising that their type should have withstood political upheavals, revolution and a change of dynasty. It was perhaps with thoughts of such a lovely little building as Mompessom House in the Salisbury Close that Horace Walpole wrote, on returning to England from Italy in 1741: "I had before discovered that there was nowhere but in England the distinction of middling people; I perceive now there is peculiar to us middling houses; how snug they are!"

Many such delightful small houses, on the edge of old villages or in the calm of cathedral cities, are honoured by an attribution to the master, but, as in the case of Inigo Jones, the majority of such can be regarded as no more than engaging myths. In West Street, Chichester, for instance, stands an excellent example sometimes known as Wren House. It was built in 1696 of brick with fine stone dressings. The slight projection that forms the central feature of the reserved frontage is entirely faced with stone, and the doorway and window above it are conceived as a single composition. The roof springs from a deeply carved cornice which surrounds the house, and many of the windows retain their wooden mullions. Groombridge Place in Kent (60) dates from the same period and is rather similar in treatment, though no stone is used. Here the traditional attribution to Wren has perhaps more substance, for he is known to have been a friend of the owner at the time of building; but the house, for all its charm, lacks the master touch. Belton House in Lincolnshire (69), on a grander scale, was begun in 1689 and has everything except proof to suggest that it is Wren's work;

67   RAYNHAM HALL, NORFOLK : the East Front, built in
1636 but later altered by William Kent

68   THE TREASURER'S HOUSE, YORK : the Green Parlour
(late 17th Century)

69 BELTON HOUSE, LINCOLNSHIRE, FROM THE SOUTH-EAST. Begun in 1684

70 SUDBURY HALL, DERBYSHIRE. Begun *circa* 1615, completed *circa* 1670

it is one of the largest and handsomest houses in the "Wren manner". The Moot in Wiltshire (8), dating from about 1690, is another smaller house delightfully characteristic of the same type, as is Heale in the same county, now enlarged, which dates from a few years earlier.

Wren, of course, was known to have employed assistants, such as the nebulous Dr. Hooke, to whom certain of his works have been attributed, and Nicholas Hawksmoor. Nevertheless, he stood unchallenged as the architectural arbiter of his age until the appearance on the scene of Vanbrugh (1663–1726) from the world of fashion and high

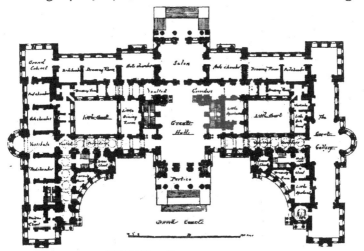

BLENHEIM: GROUND PLAN

comedy. How this audacious dramatic master acquired the knowledge and training for a crowded architectural career is still rather uncertain, but it is obvious how appropriately his stage sense was employed in service of the aristocratic megalomania of the times. The ultimate individuality of his style did not develop immediately, Castle Howard,* though conceived on a vast scale, conforms architecturally to Italian precedent; only in the layout is there a hint of the architect's theatrical vigour of conception. Blenheim Palace, begun for the first Duke of Marlborough in 1705 as a national gift, and interrupted by incessant quarrels between the architect and the termagant Duchess Sarah, shows far greater originality. The vast central block with flanking courtyards is arranged to convey the greatest possible sense of size, and the result

* Now unhappily destroyed.

is a triumph of ostentation (71). It was in the detail that
Vanbrugh displayed his lack of architectural training—sometimes coarse and heavy, as in the entrance front of Duncombe
Park (1713) (72), sometimes thin and weak, as in the eastern
façade of King's Weston (1710). Vanbrugh's whole genius
lay in his sense of the magnificent—a sense which the present
photographs contrive to catch very happily. His interest in
such a detail as domestic convenience was slight, and his
houses are reported practically uninhabitable. Yet no English
architect has displayed so true a feeling for the Baroque, and
no other hand could have produced such intensely individual
houses as Seaton Delaval (1718) (73)in Northumberland or
Grimsthorpe Castle (1723) in Lincolnshire.

Vanbrugh provides an exotic and unexpected interlude in
the story of English architecture, but it cannot be said that
his work had any permanent influence on the course of
Palladian development. Nor did Nicholas Hawksmoor (1661–
1736), who had worked under both Wren and Vanbrugh,
succeed in swinging the pendulum of taste decisively in the
direction of either one of his masters, though of the buildings
which he designed on his own account, both the fine London
churches, such as St. Mary Wolnoth, Christ Church Spital-
fields, and St. George's Bloomsbury, and the mansions, such
as Easton Neston in Northamptonshire, with its high pilas-
tered façades and deep cornice, are perhaps most reminiscent
of Vanbrugh. But a third contemporary of Wren's was working on more individual lines. This was William Talman, a
Dutchman, whose work enjoyed a considerable vogue in this
country. Besides assisting Wren at Hampton Court, he
designed Chatsworth (74) for the first Duke of Devonshire
in 1687 and Dyrham Park in Gloucestershire a few years later.
The former, which was twenty years in building, narrowly
fails to be a masterpiece. Built of a beautiful local stone in
the form of a hollow rectangle, the design has all the merits
of dignity and simplicity. From a heavily rusticated lower
storey pilasters rise to a cornice embellished with heraldic
designs; above is a pierced parapet surmounted by stone
urns. For reasons still obscure Talman placed his magnificent
suite of reception rooms on the second, and top, floor of the
house; thus, the upper windows are considerably larger than
those below them and produce an uncomfortable effect.
Further, the keystones of all the windows, particularly those
of the top floor which are carved with the Cavendish crest,
are so massive that they seem to weigh down the gilded

71 BLENHEIM PALACE, OXFORDSHIRE (1715). By Sir John Vanbrugh.
The East Façade with the new Formal Garden beneath

72 DUNCOMBE PARK, YORKSHIRE : the Entrance Front. Begun in 1713 ; Sir John Vanbrugh, Architect

73 SEATON DELAVAL, NORTHUMBERLAND: the Entrance Front, begun *circa* 1718; Sir John Vanbrugh, Architect. The House now stands vacant and partly derelict in an industrial district

74 CHATSWORTH, DERBYSHIRE, FROM THE SOUTH (begun in 1687). William Talman, Architect. On the Left are Wyattville's additions of the early 19th Century

sashes. For the noble rooms within there can be nothing but praise; the house contains the finest Stuart *suite* in England (82). Dyrham, begun in 1698, is less ambitious both in size and design; indeed the façades rather lack inspiration, and have an urban and insipid air.

At the dawn of Palladianism the planning and furnishing of houses had already undergone great changes. The traditional hall of the Middle Ages had at last been discarded, though it was to continue to make occasional and surprising appearances, as at Easton Neston, which dates from 1702, where the main features of the layout are almost medieval. The enterprising and observant Mrs. Celia Fiennes, in the course of her *Rides through England on a Side Saddle* during the years immediately before and after 1700, describes very adequately the usual planning of a country house of that date. Her description of the "fine house of Sir George Pratt's called Coalsell" (designed as has already been observed by Sir Roger Pratt about 1650) will serve as a model. "The house is new built of stone, most of ye offices are partly under ground—kitchen, Pantry, buttlery and good Cellers and round a Court is all ye other offices & out houses; The entrance of ye house is an ascent of severall steps into a hall, so lofty the rooff is three storyes, reaches to ye floore of ye gallery—all the walls are Cutt in hollows where statues & Heads Carved ffinely are sett, Directly fore-right Enters a large Dineing roome or great parlour, which has a door thourough into the garden yt. gives a visto through ye house: within yt. is a drawing room, on ye other side another roome of the same size, and backward is a little parlour all with good ffurniture, tapistry, Damaske, etc. . . . on the tope of the stairs you enter in ye midde into a dineing roome, within that a Chamber on each side with two closets to each bigg Enough for a little bed, with chimney's convenient for a servant and for dressing roomes, one of which has a doore also out into that passage and soe to the back staire . . . They are all well and Genteel'ly furnisht, damaskes Chamlet and wrought beds ffashionable made up. Over this runs a Gallery all through the house, and on each sid severall garret roomes for servants ffurnished very neate and Genteele, in ye middle are staires yt lead up to the Cupilow or large Lanthorn in the middle of the leads" . . . She noted that "there was few pictures in the house only over doores and Chimney's". This was a relief after Burghley, which she so admirably summed up as "Eminent for its Curiosity", where she took some exception to the paintings, "very fine paint in pictures, but they were all without Garments or very little, that was the only fault, ye immodesty of ye Pictures, Especially in My Lords appartment".

Interior decoration during the later Stuart period was entirely the work of the architect, and the upholsterer was as yet seldom allowed to intervene. Floors were now sometimes inlaid with different coloured woods in a manner called Parquetage, and panels of inlay were introduced over fire-places, as in the state rooms at Chatsworth. In other cases the floor was simply covered with rush matting, the carpets, brought from the East together with choice Chinese porcelain by the ships of the East India Company, being used to drape the tables. As early as the reign of Charles I paper and leather hangings had been used as wall-coverings, while the rich imported tapestries and pictures by the Continental masters or, for the most important rooms, engaged foreign artists to paint suitably stimulating scenes on the ceilings. But the more usual wall-covering, for bedrooms and sitting-rooms alike, was a simple wood panelling as a protection against cold and damp. This might be made either of oak, cedar or pine, but the latter, when used, was generally either painted a plain colour, or grained to represent oak, as in the library at Raby Castle, Durham, and the King's dining-room at Drayton House. The designs could differ considerably, but the average architect remained faithful to the large oblong panel of an earlier age. The work could be very simple, as in the dining-room at Holme Lacey in Herefordshire, which dates from about 1694, where the particularly broad panels are made up of several pieces and surrounded by a deep molding, the only relief being a chair-rail and a carved cornice. There is rather similar wainscoting in the Oak Room at Balls Park which dates from nearly fifty years earlier, but in this case the panels are much narrower. In the Balcony Room at Dyrham (*circa* 1698) the panels are separated by Ionic pilasters supporting a full entablature, and the whole is painted a warm brown with gilded enrichments.

In the years following the Restoration, many marbles were imported for the first time into England from Italy and Ireland, and these were used for the heavy bolection moldings placed around fireplace openings, as in the state apartments at Chatsworth. Immediately over the opening was usually an oblong mirror, and above this a picture surrounded by a

70 FORDE ABBEY, DORSET: in the Large Drawing-room, attributed to Inigo Jones (mid-17th Century)

75 KNOLE, KENT: in the King's Bedroom, showing the Silver Furniture and Tapestries fitted for James I

78 CASTLE ASHBY, NORTHAMPTONSHIRE:
the early 17th-Century Staircase

77 DUNSTER CASTLE, SOMERSET : the Great
Staircase (*circa* 1681)

molding and raised from the plane of the wall in the same manner as the compartments of panelling. The most elaborate decoration was confined to the plaster ceiling. Its design was generally based on a fairly formal plan, consisting, perhaps, of a large central panel in high relief surrounded by lesser geometric figures in a layout rather akin to that of a Stuart garden. Within this broad scheme a considerable license was allowed. Flowers, leaves and fruit were displayed in great opulence and abandon, and lurking among the clustered wreaths might be discovered groups of birds, as at Melton Constable in Norfolk (1687), *putti*, as at Brickwall in Sussex (1685), fish as (appropriately enough) at the New River Company's office (1690), or even a cartouche of musical instruments, as at Denham Place in Buckinghamshire (1693). But in an aristocratic age the most usual culmination was the crest, or occasionally the full coat of arms, of the owner.

Undoubtedly the greatest individual craftsmen of this period was Grinling Gibbons (1648–1721) who, with his assistants, produced carving of a lightness and beauty never surpassed, though his naturalistic representations of flowers, fruit, birds and even lace are sometimes more remarkable for their technical virtuosity than for the quality of their design. Some of his finest work was executed for the quire of St. Paul's, but much is also to be found among the great houses of the age. The Carved Room at Petworth (81), where the swags of flowers and fruits are interspersed with musical instruments and Greek urns, is perhaps his supreme domestic achievement. Much fine carving adorns the chimney-pieces and panelling of English country houses "in the Grinling Gibbons manner", clearly only a fraction of which could have been the work of the master. It speaks much for the craftsmanship of the day that work of this standard could have been produced by what in most cases were probably no more than provincial journeymen whose names have seldom survived. One such, however, has come down to us, that of Samuel Watson, a Derbyshire man, who carried out the magnificent carving in the state-rooms at Chatsworth around 1691. His work has not, perhaps, the delicacy of detail of Petworth or Holme Lacey (now removed), but the general effect at least is as rich and splendid as anything produced by Gibbons.

In 1677 the manufacture of Gobelin tapestry was begun in France, and specimens soon began to decorate English walls.

A few years later M. Marquet began to make his beautiful furniture inlaid with different coloured woods, which came to be known as *marqueterie* and achieved a considerable vogue in this country. Early in the reign of Queen Anne the native manufacture of wallpapers was embarked upon, a type of covering often found more economical as well as more cheerful in the high rooms of the period, where panelling had hitherto almost exclusively been used. This innovation was advertised in the press, and the following announcement from the *Postman* of 1702 gives an idea of the large variety of designs. "At the Blue Paper Warehouse in Aldermanbury (and nowhere else) in London, are sold the true sorts of figur'd Paper Hangings, some in pieces of 12 yards long, others after the manner of real Tapistry, others in imitation of Irish stitch, flower'd Damasks, Sprigs and Branches, others in yard wide, Emboss'd work, and a curious sort of Flock Work in imitation of Caffaws, and other Hangings of curious figures and colours. As also Linnen Cloath, Tapestry Hangings, with a variety of Skreens and Chimney pieces, and sashes for windows, as transparent as sarconet." Another offers "imitation of Marbles and other coloured wainscoats, which are to be put into Pannels and Mouldings made for that purpose, fit for the hanging of Parlours, Dining rooms and Staircases; and others in Yard wide Emboss'd work, in imitation of Gilded Leather". Here clearly was a precedent for the popular "Lincrusta" of late-Victorian times. But the most sought-after papers were those brought from China which were painted with flowers and birds in brilliant colours, some few of which, to our great good fortune, have survived. They were usually considered only suitable for bedrooms, and later in the century were found to make excellent backgrounds for Mr. Chippendale's furniture in the Chinese taste.

The painting of walls and ceilings, usually with allegorical scenes, became increasingly popular in great houses during the reigns of William III and Anne. At Burghley, for example, in the words of Mrs. Fiennes, there were "at least 20 rooms, very large and lofty that are all painted on the top". Verrio and Laguerre, two minor executants in the Baroque manner, were the foreign artists most in demand, and their work can be seen in houses all over the country. It was not until the appearance of Sir James Thornhill (1676–1734) that an English artist was found to compete with them, the best specimens of whose work may be seen in the dome of St. Paul's Cathedral

79 QUENBY HALL, LEICESTERSHIRE : a panelled Bedroom
of *circa* 1600

81 PETWORTH HOUSE, SUSSEX: the Carved Room, executed by
Grinling Gibbons and his Assistants in the late 17th Century

and the Painted Hall at Greenwich, for which he was remuner-
ated at the rate of forty shillings a square yard. Domestic
examples exist at Blenheim Palace, Charborough Park in
Dorset, Hanbury Hall, Worcestershire, and (until its recent
gutting by fire) Stoke Edith in Herefordshire, among other
houses. But to-day Thornhill's chief claim to distinction is as
the master and later father-in-law of Hogarth.

Rooms of the Carolean and William and Mary periods
would appear from pictures to have been rather sparsely furnished. The cupboards and commodes were inlaid with ivory
and coloured woods in intricate patterns, the familiar straight-
backed chairs being richly carved between their cane panels.
In the reign of Anne walnut grew to be the fashionable
material for furniture, the angular lines of the previous reigns
giving way to the restrained curves and cabriole legs of
this most famous of English "periods". The invaluable
Celia Fiennes carefully describes Queen Anne's rooms at
Windsor:

> "On the right hand is a large Antyroome for persons to wait,
> where are Marble tables in ye Peeres between the windows;
> white damaske window curtaines and cane chairs. Next it
> is the Dinneing rooms some steppes down, where was red
> silk curtaines Chaires and Stooles, and Benches round the
> room all red silk, with some coulld. orrice Lace, here was
> a white marble table behind the doore as a sideboard, and a
> Clap table under ye Large Looking Glass between the windows.
> Next this was a drawing roome; both these roomes were hung
> with small Image tapistry very Lively and ffresh, here was
> Crimson Damaske window Curtaines, Chaires and stooles.
> The next was what was Prince George's dressing roome,
> hung, and window Curtaines Chaires and stooles, all with
> yellow damasks, with marble chimney pieces as all ye Roomes
> have of Differing Coullrs. black, white and grey rance etc.,
> etc. Large Looking-glasses, all the roomes in all ye house
> is plaine unvarnished oake Wainscoate which Lookes very
> neate."

The most sumptuous and important piece of furniture
remained the bed. The squat, bulbous four-posters of the
Tudors gave way to beds of greater height and elegance.
The tester was supported on tall, slender pillars and was
often hung with stuffs of great richness. A splendid example
is the bed hung with gold and silver tissue in the King's
Bedroom at Knole which was made for a visit of James II
and is said to have cost £8,000. A complete silver toilet set

K

was made for the same occasion at a cost of many further thousands; and a bed chamber at Burghley about 1700 was "ffurnish'd very Rich, the tapistry was all blew Silke and Rich Gold thread, so that the Gold appeared for ye Light part of all the worke. There was a blew velvet bed with gold ffringe and very Richly Embroidered, all the Inside with ovals on the head piece and tester, where are so finely wrought in Satten stitch it looks Like painting." In other rooms "there was at least 4 velvet beds 2 plaine and 2 figured— Crimson-green. Several Coullours together in one; severall Damaske beds and some tissue beds all ffinely Embroydered."

The bedroom was the scene of the most extravagant displays of mourning. A bereaved husband or wife was expected to hang his walls with black, while the bed was draped with heavy black cloth and decorated with black plumes, even the coverlet being of the same colour. So rigid was this custom that a young Verney widow had to be excused to her relatives for having a white counterpane "because she is sick and cannot bear black cloth". These great mourning beds were sent round the family on the appropriate occasions, and the loan of the family bed was considered a considerable solace to the bereaved, though one might have supposed its presence would rather have served to emphasise the loss.

Under the Tudors, the number and variety of the servants employed in the households of the newly enriched had been prodigious—a regular incentive to the attacks of satirists and moralists. Even after the Restoration, when the whole country still suffered from the privations of the Civil War and Interregnum, there was little diminution in the quantity of persons employed by a great provincial landlord. That a good number was required for the running of the immense inconvenient houses of the period cannot be doubted, particularly as the function of male servants was not entirely menial but included the duties of guards and escorts when travelling. Nevertheless, the primary purpose of these menservants was ostentation, to impress the onlooker by their number and the splendour of their liveries. The affected footman was as much a butt for satirists in late-Stuart and early-Georgian times as in the pages of *Punch* during the reign of Queen Victoria; but he could afford to smile superciliously in the face of criticism, for the "vails" expected and generally received for the smallest services were on an exorbitant scale compared with nowadays. Steele devotes a whole edition of *The Spectator* to the subject of menservants:

82 CHATSWORTH, DERBYSHIRE : the State Bedroom. One of a splendid Suite of Interiors designed by William Talman in 1687

83 HOLME LACY, HEREFORDSHIRE: the Yellow Dressing-room.
A pleasing Interior of *circa* 1680

"They are but in a lower Degree what their masters themselves are; . . . you have Liveries, Beaux, Fops, and coxcombs, in as high perfection, as among people that keep Equipages." And elsewhere "There is nothing we Beaux take more Pride in than a Sett of Genteel Footmen; I never have any but what wear their own hair, and I allow 'em a Crown a Week for Gloves and Powder".

Addison in the same periodical records another duty for the manservant. "I remember the time when some of our well-bred County Women kept their *Valet de Chambre*, because, forsooth, a man was much more handy about them than one of their own Sex. I myself have seen one of these male *Abigails* tripping about the Room with a looking glass in his hand, and combing his Lady's Hair a whole morning together."

Another feature of the Stuart and early-Georgian household was the black servant, who, besides striking a fashionably exotic note, was also something of an economy since as a slave he required no pay. He had a tiresome habit, however, of trying to give the slip to his indulgent master, and advertisements such as the following were quite common: "A slender middle sized India Black, in a dark grey Livery with Brass Buttons, went from Mrs. Thwaits, in Stepney, the 4th of June." Or "A Negro Maid, aged about 16 yrs, much pitted with the Small Pox, speaks English well, having a piece of her left ear bit off by a dog; she hath on a strip'd stuff waistcoat and Petticoat". Or again "A Tall Negro young fellow commonly known as Jack Chelsea, having a Collar about his Neck, with these words, Mr. Mosey Goodyeare of Chelsea, his Negro".

Side by side with opulence and grandeur went the squalor resulting from lack of sanitation. Sir John Harington's ingenious invention of the water-closet during the reign of Elizabeth had fallen upon an unappreciative public. The medieval privy had given way to a simple slop-pail, which, however adequate for country use, was distinctly unsuitable for the town, where it was generally simply emptied out of the window into the street. The stench of London, particularly in summer, was almost insupportable; Pepys describes how he was driven indoors one fine evening by "the stink of shying a shitten pot".

Early in the eighteenth century, however, a drainage system of sorts was evolved. Pipes and cess-pools became fairly usual in country houses; Isaac Ware shows a plan on which the lines of the drains are indicated, and mentions an improved drainage system built beneath the Horse Guards. Nevertheless the "closet" remained persistently scarce in great houses. In Kent's plan, dated 1734, of the vast *piano nobile* of Holkham, for instance, there is only one, and that without a window, tucked away in an odd corner formed by the apse of the hall. It had the merit, however, of being arranged as a double contrivance, seating two at a time, as may still be seen in remote farmhouses to-day. It was much the same in James Paine's plan for Kedleston twenty-five years later, though there the single closet could at least boast a window. Robert Adam, however, generally allowed a more generous supply. In the plan dated 1771 for Luton Hoo there were to have been four on the principal floor, and a moderate-sized house designed in the same year for Mr. Baron Mure was even better equipped. But Harewood and Sion, dating respectively from 1759 and 1761, had only one apiece.

As early as the reign of Queen Anne there was at Windsor, however, an up-to-date arrangement consisting of "a little place with a seate of Easement of Marble with sluices of water to wash all down".

In the towns, a drainage system was more difficult to instal, and seventeenth-century methods long persisted. By the middle of the eighteenth century "the needful edifice" was usually erected in a corner of the garden, as it is to this day at Carlyle's House in Cheyne Row, Chelsea. In the country it often took the form of a small garden temple, as at the fine brick rectory of Pertenhall near Kimbolton. At the same time bathrooms were not unknown; Celia Fiennes, with her usual thoroughness, inspected the very elaborate "Batheing roome" at Chatsworth, "ye walls all with blew and white marble—the pavement mix'd, one stone white, another black, another of ye Red vaned marble. The bath is one Entire marble all white finely veined with blew . . . It was deep as ones middle on the outside, and ye went down steps into ye bath big enough for two people. At ye upper End are two locks to let in one hott, ye other Cold water to attemper it as persons please—the Windows are all private Glass." Again at Holkham in 1773 there was a bathroom supplied with hot water pumped up from the basement.

In most directions the amenities of life steadily improved in the years following the Restoration. The meals of the rich, though still rather crude and coarse in the eyes of the more fastidious French, had assumed less gluttonous proportions.

The long dining tables were covered with white cloths; the guests sat round on tapestried stools, high-backed chairs being reserved for visitors of the greatest importance. Cutlery was rarely provided, and guests were expected to bring their own spoons. Forks were only slowly coming into use and were wielded by the English with an abandon which horrified Continental visitors. They were poked at random into any dish and, most distressing of all, were often employed for picking teeth. Ewers for washing the fingers, which were customary in France, were seldom provided, but one large basin was produced into which all dipped hands and napkins. But habits changed quickly, and by the middle of the eighteenth century the manners of the fashionable world were, on the whole, as impeccable, more or less, as they are to-day.

The important meal of the day was dinner, which was eaten by the middle classes at two o'clock but by the fashionable world an hour or two later; references to breakfast or supper are seldom found. Misson, a Frenchman, who travelled in England during the reign of Queen Anne, gave a critical account of the English and their food.

"The English eat a great deal at dinner, they rest a while, and to it again, till they have quite stuff'd their Paunch. Their Supper is moderate: Gluttons at noon, and abstinent at Night. I heard always they were great Flesh eaters, and I have found it true . . . There are some Noblemen that have both *French* and *English* cooks, and these eat much after the *French* manner; but among the middling Sort of People they have ten or twelve Sorts of common meats, which infallibly take their turns at their Tables, and two Dishes are their Dinners: a Pudding, for instance, and a Piece of Roast Beef; another time they will have a piece of boil'd beef, and then they salt it some Days beforehand, and besiege it with five or six Heaps of Cabbage, Carrots, Turnips or some other Herbs or Roots, well pepper'd and salted and swimming in butter: A Leg of roast or boil'd Mutton, dish'd up with the same dainties, Fowls, Pigs, Ox Tripes, and Tongues, Rabbits, Pidgeons, all well moistened with Butter, without larding."

The cooking sounds strangely familiar except that, in this more economical age, water has supplanted butter.

The one dish for which Misson had nothing but praise was the Pudding; after describing its various forms he concludes with a little panegyric:

"Blessed be he who invented Pudding, for it is a Manna that hits the Palates of all sorts of People; ah, what an excellent thing is the English Pudding."

The raw materials for food were probably finer in England at this time than anywhere in Europe. Cattle and pigs fattened on the rich pastures and flocks of sheep on the chalk downs; the supply of milk and cream was abundant. In the forests and marshes deer and many other sorts of game were plentiful; the standard of living of the common people was remarkably high, and the natural resources of the country more than adequate to supply the needs of the five million odd who in 1680 made up the population. Beer and ale remained the national drinks except in the western counties where cider took their place; in addition, large quantities of foreign wines were imported for the gentry. The consumption of alcohol was immense in all classes, the regulation allowance of beer for a common sailor being as much as a gallon a day.

In 1676 a tax of twopence a quart had been put on wine in order to pay the King's debts, and Sir Ralph Verney rejoiced, "for if the people have noe Minde to pay this Tax, let them be drunk with ale and strong Beere. I beleeve Brandy will be forbid, or so great a Tax layd on it that none will import it: for since Labouring men have got a Trick of drinking Brandy, 'tis evident it hath hindred the Brewing of many hundred thousand quarters of Mault in England." This tax brought in a considerable revenue owing to the efforts of patriotic gentlemen who "take their three bottles of French claret every night because it brings a great custom to the Crown". But their patriotism was not without its drawbacks, and "I look'd to have found you with your head ake and your morning Qualms" was a not unusual salutation.

Although during the wars with France the market was still well supplied, by the devious methods of smugglers, with French wines, it was not considered patriotic to drink them; thus Port acquired a great popularity among gentlefolk. This taste was highly commended by Steele who wrote in *The Spectator*: "a bottle or two of good solid Edifying Port, made a Night cheerful, and threw off Reserve. But this plaguy French Claret will not only cost us more money but do us less good."

Whatever accusations may be levelled against the England

84 DITCHLEY, OXFORDSHIRE (*circa* 1722). Built by James Gibbs on the site of the older House of the Restoration Poet, Rochester

85 HOUGHTON HALL, NORFOLK, FROM THE SOUTH-EAST.
Colin Campbell, Architect, *circa* 1722

86 VEN HOUSE, SOMERSET: the Garden Front (1700)

of Anne and the first Georges, that of sobriety should not be among them. The rows of self-indulgent faces that gaze down at us loftily from beneath capacious periwigs on the walls of innumerable English country houses tell their own tale of a license that has left its gouty legacy through many generations of Englishmen, even to our own days.

CHAPTER IV

THE CULT OF THE ANTIQUE
(*Circa* 1720 to 1850)

THE natural urge of the English towards building is never long suppressed, and generally makes its reappearance as prosperity returns to the country. During the early and middle years of the seventeenth century the resources of the upper classes had, on the whole, been far too depleted for much activity in this sphere, but with the dawn of a period of agricultural prosperity (for the rich at least) at the opening of the eighteenth century, English landlords were able to indulge themselves in a small orgy of building which the wars of the reign of Queen Anne hardly seemed to check. An immense enthusiasm for architecture now permeated the upper classes No young man's education was considered complete until he had acquired at least some smattering of the mistress art, while the Grand Tour, that inevitable climax to the education of a young gentleman of position and hallmark of social status, was devoted as much to the study of the architectural masterpieces of the Continent as to the acquisition of poise and polish in the world of manners.

This amateur cult of knowledge, so admirable a thing in itself, was destined to have a somewhat sterilising effect on architectural development in this country. No longer could the evolution of style be left to the natural impulse of the builder; under the influence of fashion it became a more complex and self-conscious process. The traditional vernacular, which had so easily withstood the surface elaboration of the Early Renaissance and even the cultured innovations of Inigo Jones and Webb, had found a new vitality at the hands of Wren and his followers—a vitality which, had it been left to develop on its own lines, might well have produced one of the most gracious and distinctive schools of Renaissance practice. As it was, the pendulum of fashion was allowed to swing once more in the Palladian direction; Wren was of set purpose ignored, and Jones and his master came again, after a lapse of half a century, to be regarded as the oracles of English taste. Kent published his *Designs of Inigo Jones* in 1727, and the Palladian movement was embarked on its triumphant second career.

87 GILLING CASTLE, YORKSHIRE: the West End of the Gallery
(early 18th Century)

58 HOLKHAM HALL, NORFOLK (1734). By William Kent.
The Dining-room

At its best it was a gracious style, admirably adapted to the social requirements of the rich; and even to-day it is remarkable how its products, founded upon the showy splendours of Vicenza, adapt themselves to the cooler climate of the English country. As a movement it was carried forward on a surge of amateur enthusiasm and activity, but professional architects were quick to adapt themselves to the needs of patrons, and a "school" came into being with extraordinary rapidity. The animating spirit was Richard Boyle, Earl of Burlington (1695-1753), an "amateur" of genuine talent and vision, a man of wealth and position and a munificent patron of the arts. This cultured Maecenas, surrounded by his eager band: Campbell, Leoni, Kent, with Palladio as their god, Jones as their prophet and *The Book of Architecture* as their bible: may be allowed the credit for first inoculating English architecture with the virus of revival that was to be at once its weakness and its charm. Nøt content merely to emulate Palladio's severe forms, they sometimes went so far as to adopt his actual plans; thus both Mereworth Castle in Kent, designed by Colin Campbell about 1720, and Chiswick Villa, designed by Burlington with the assistance of Kent some seven years later, were closely modelled on the Villa Capra at Vicenza. The design, though well suited to the abundant sunshine of the Plain of Lombardy, seemed less happy among the English hedgerows, consisting as it did of a central circular hall rising high into a dome (from the windows in which came the only light), while around it were grouped the reception rooms, the whole forming on plan a compact square. At Mereworth, the nearest of the two to the original, there is a deeply-projecting portico in the centre of each façade, so that the majority of the outer rooms are denied direct sunlight. At Chiswick the porticoes were discarded except on the entrance side, but only in this respect is it superior to its twin, for with its small scale and crowded detail the effect is amusing rather than architecturally satisfactory. Campbell produced far sounder work when clinging less desperately to Palladian precedent. Houghton Hall in Norfolk (85), for instance, which he designed for Prime Minister Walpole about 1720, consisting of a substantial central block with a dome at each corner supported by pavilions connected with the house by long arcades, has real strength and individuality of design, and suffers from none of that deadness that is the inevitable corollary of close copy. Campbell will always be remembered as the compiler of the first three volumes of

L

Vitruvius Britannicus, an inaccurate, partial but nevertheless extremely interesting illustrative record of domestic building during the earlier eighteenth century.

Campbell, though something of a slave to architectural fashion, achieved in his buildings an "anglicisation" of Palladianism that contrasts with the more polished and Italianate manner of Giacomo Leoni. Leoni (*circa* 1686-1746) was in fact a Venetian brought to London by Burlington to assist in the preparation of an edition of the works of Palladio, but he soon acquired an English practice, among his major works being the stately Moor Park in Hertfordshire and the south front of Lyme Park in Cheshire (94), both completed about 1720. Leoni had more virtuosity, more certainty of touch, perhaps, than Campbell, qualities that appear triumphantly in these two houses; nevertheless there is something lacking that the less accomplished Englishmen could often provide: a warmth, a humanity, a sympathy for the surroundings. If the Italians could build palaces for princes, it was the supreme talent of the English architects that their houses supplied fitting accommodation for country gentlemen.

A rather clumsy bleakness was perhaps the worst error into which the English Palladians were prone to fall. Ditchley in Oxfordshire (84) and Sudbrooke Park near Richmond, both designed by James Gibbs (1689-1754), show something of this tendency in the paucity of their external decoration and the grimness of their outlines, while much the same criticism can be made of the vast houses of Henry Flitcroft (1697-1769)— Wentworth Woodhouse in Yorkshire (89) and Woburn Abbey in Bedfordshire—and of the work of Isaac Ware. Even William Kent (1684-1748), the most brilliant of Burlington's band, was not always above criticism in this respect. If the Horse Guards in Whitehall is a work of consummate skill and refinement, the exterior of Holkham in Norfolk (which was completed by Brettingham after his death) carries austerity to surprising lengths (98). Built of white brick, with thin cornices and shallow stone pediments, superficial ornament is entirely lacking and the whole effect is only saved from active ugliness by the excellence of the proportions. Perhaps, one feels, Kent deliberately struck this grim external note to enhance the interior magnificence of the reception rooms, which are among the finest of the eighteenth century and still, fortunately, embellished by the original splendid if monumental furniture (88).

So much is heard throughout the earlier eighteenth century

89 WENTWORTH WOODHOUSE, YORKSHIRE, showing the vast extent of the Entrance Front.

90   KIRTLINGTON PARK, OXFORDSHIRE, FROM THE SOUTH-WEST.   A Palladian design of 1742

of the fashionable architect and his larger products that one is apt to forget that other work was done. As a matter of fact builders all over the country had never been more active in raising "middling" houses for the smaller squires and members of the rising professional classes. However remotely situated from the capital, the country builder could now keep in constant touch with metropolitan development by subscribing to the stream of architectural pattern-books that began to flow at this time. With the aid of these, a competent artisan could erect a building from basement to attic without a single original idea of his own; all the necessary information was supplied in elevation and plan, down to the detail of doorways, staircases and chimney-pieces.

In view of this it remains something of a mystery that the smaller Palladian house is such a rarity; for the pattern-books, with hardly an exception, were dogmatically Palladian in principle. But the fact remains that throughout most of the eighteenth century country builders persisted in the pleasant tradition established by Wren, in the quiet dignity of their productions in brick or stone largely eschewing the vicissitudes of metropolitan fashion until their manner became submerged beneath the facile stucco of the Regency. Thus the Wren vernacular lingered unobtrusively in country places side by side with the productions of Palladianism and of the Classic Revival, and has happily set its seal upon the architecture of many villages and most country towns. Despite the undoubted popularity enjoyed by the pattern-books, such compact Palladian examples as Boreham House in Essex and Great Marlow Place must be taken as the exception rather than as the rule.

The most prolific of the pattern-book writers was the highly unsuccessful architect Batty Langley (1696-1751), who though apparently somewhat incompetent as a practical designer, was the author of innumerable books on the art and practice of building, which had an immense sale. He was closely rivalled in popularity by several others, such as Robert Morris, the designer of Inveraray Castle in Argyllshire, who produced manuals from 1736 on, some written alone and some in conjunction with William and John Halfpenny, "architects and carpenters"; while with T. Lightoler, "carver", he issued a *Modern Builder's Assistant* which entered exhaustively into every conceivable detail of house construction. William Pain, who entered the field a little later, was second only to Langley in his fecundity of ouptut. *The Builders'*

Pocket Treasure of 1763 was followed by a procession of volumes of which the last, *The Practical House Carpenter*, appeared as late as 1790. Isaac Ware in 1756 published his *Complete Body of Architecture* in which, incidentally, he strongly advocated the use of yellow or grey brick in preference to red, which he considered "fiery and disagreeable to the eye . . . and most improper in the country". Light-coloured stock brick enjoyed, indeed, a considerable vogue during the middle years of the century. Kent had used it, as has been seen, at Holkham; his example was followed later by Holland at Broadlands and Althorp (102). Nevertheless, its popularity would now seem hardly justified, and the years have had little softening effect on its hard, uncompromising sheen.

Mrs. Delany (then Pendarves) writing from Ireland in 1731 gives an interesting description of the interior arrangement of a country house at this time: "First there is a very good hall well filled with servants, then a room of 18 foot square, wainscoted with oak, the panels all carved, and the doors and chimney finished with a very fine high carving, the ceiling stucco, the window curtains and chairs yellow Genoa damask, portraits and landscapes, very well done, round the room, marble tables between the windows, and looking-glasses with gilt frames. The next room is 28 ft. long and 22 broad, and is as finely adorned as damask, pictures, and busts can make it, besides the floor being covered with the finest Persian carpet that ever was seen." And there was another house which she described as *magnifique*: "the apartments are handsome, and furnished with gold coloured damask—virtues, and busts, and pictures that the bishop brought with him from Italy. A universal cheerfulness reigns in the house. They keep a very handsome table, six dishes of meat are constantly at dinner, and six plates at supper." She follows with an account of the smooth passing of a day: "We meet at breakfast about ten, chocolate, tea, coffee, toast and butter, and caudle etc., are devoured without mercy. The hall is so large that very often breakfast, battledore and shuttlecock, and the harpsichord, go on at the *same time* without molesting one another . . . . Yesterday we walked 4 miles before dinner, and danced two hours in the evening, we have very good music for that purpose; at nine we have prayers, and afterwards till supper is on the table the organ or harpsichord is engaged."

Mrs. Delany's description gives some impression of the ordinary richness of the Palladian interior. The most important

91 HOUGHTON HALL, NORFOLK: Sir Robert Walpole's Library.
Colin Campbell, Architect, *circa* 1722

93 CROOME COURT, WORCESTERSHIRE: the South Front
(*circa* 1750). A Remodelling by Robert Adam

94 LYME HALL, CHESHIRE: the South Front.
By Giacomo Leoni (1726-32)

95   EDGCOTE, NORTHAMPTONSHIRE.   Built between 1748 and 1753

96   HONINGTON HALL, WARWICKSHIRE (begun *circa* 1680).   Notice
the effective use of classical busts in niches as decoration

97   MOOR PARK, HERTFORDSHIRE : a Corner of the Great Hall.
By Giacomo Leoni (*circa* 1720)

room was usually the hall, often a high rectangular apartment with a gallery at the first floor level, as at Houghton, Moor Park (97) and Wentworth Woodhouse. The doorways would be treated very architecturally, carved in stone or marble and flanked by columns supporting a cornice and pediment, the latter often surmounted by figures; while the plaster decoration of walls and ceiling might be carried out by Italian craftsmen in the most riotous style of their native country. At Moor Park the walls are designed to take large canvases, the frames of which are supported by cupids and fish-tailed children. At Houghton the treatment is slightly more restrained, with large busts in niches and square plaques between the heavy stone doorways. On the ceiling, however, invention runs riot. Armies of *amorini* dance, play, chase one another and swing on the rich garlands around the cove, occasionally lowering an erring leg over the cornice. These are but two examples among many in an age of flamboyant plasterwork; such houses as Hagley, Kirtlington (90), Honington (96), furnish equally exuberant schemes. Of a somewhat different category, however, was the marble hall at Holkham, perhaps the finest interior built during the eighteenth century in this country, which Kent modelled on the form of a Roman basilica. Along each side is a raised arcade of fluted alabaster columns, while a long flight of steps leads up opposite the entrance to the door of the saloon in the apse. The whole conception is of a magnificence that is something more than an expression of provincial dignity.

Apart from the hall, the other reception rooms—saloons, libraries, withdrawing rooms—were generally of a rather homelier and more English character. The walls, from chair-rail to cornice, would probably be hung either with tapestries or red and green velvet, as at Holkham and Houghton. Chimney-pieces were rather monumental and generally designed with pedimented overmantels containing pictures, mirrors or carved plaques, as in the hall at Godmersham in Kent. Smaller houses, however, remained faithful to simple panelling; in many cases, such as Rainham Hall in Essex, almost every room was wainscoted, the only decoration, beyond a simple cornice and mantelpiece, being a recessed niche with shelves for the exhibition of china.

At this active period of taste architectural enthusiasm was far too urgent to stand still. Kent, the most brilliant member of the Burlingtonian school, died before the middle of the century, and already fashion was seeking out new fields. At the same time foreign travel was becoming less hazardous, and as Turkish power decayed in the Mediterranean, the scope of the Grand Tour could be vastly extended. Antiquaries were searching for the exciting remnants of classical civilisations; Stuart and Revett were busy at Athens, Wood and Dawkins at Palmyra and Baalbec, while in 1754 a young Scottish architect, Robert Adam, set out with his companions to make a methodical exploration of the ruins of Spalato. The erudition of the upper classes was immensely stimulated by these researches. The impulse towards classical revival that had first manifested itself in the enthusiasms of Burlington and his circle now became keener and more literal, and the aims of English architects became increasingly identified with the ancient splendours.

The new trends of taste were admirably stimulated and canalised by Adam and his brother James, whose remarkable practical ability was supported by an erudition far superior to that of most of their contemporaries. Under their leadership English classicism was quickly to lose that touch of the amateurish which had been conspicuous in many of the earlier productions of the century. Such a house as Nostell Priory in Yorkshire is characteristic of the improved technique. In 1735 James Paine had designed a bleak rectangular building for Sir Rowland Winn, the only ornamentation of its façade being a top-heavy pediment supported on five engaged columns. Forty years later Robert Adam added a north wing that was a complete composition in itself, with a well-balanced projecting portico, Ionic pilasters and columns and graceful bands of ornament, which, though to a certain extent reflecting Paine's work, had the effect of making it appear boorish and clumsy in the extreme. It was not surprising that in an age of wealth and informed taste Adam should have acquired such a vogue as no architect had enjoyed before him. But perhaps his greatest talent lay in his lively and inventive planning in which sphere he showed himself vastly superior to any of his predecessors. Behind his symmetrical façades the rooms assumed every variety of graceful shape; apses, arcades and columns so diversified them that there were seldom two alike in any of his greater houses. One has only to contrast the Adam method with that employed by such an architect as Sir Robert Taylor at Gorhambury, for instance, where the rooms are arranged like a sequence of large quadrangular boxes, to appreciate this extraordinary inventiveness, which has, perhaps, its later

98 HOLKHAM HALL, NORFOLK (begun in 1734). William Kent, Architect. An Air-view, showing the vast extent of the Lay-out

99 KEDLESTON, DERBYSHIRE: the South Façade.
Robert Adam, Architect, 1765

100 HACKNESS HALL, YORKSHIRE: the Garden Front. John Carr
of York, Architect, *circa* 1750

musical counterpart in the melodic ingenuities of Johann Strauss.

Kedleston in Derbyshire (3, 99) may be singled out as the supreme domestic achievement of Adam's career. Here, as later at Nostell, he was called in to succeed James Paine about 1763, designing the south front, the interior decoration and the greater part of the furniture even down to the detail of the fire-irons. Few more beautiful interiors were produced during the eighteenth century than the vast hall with its monolith columns of Derbyshire alabaster, the graceful rotunda that fills the central feature of the south front, the lovely living-rooms hung with pale-blue damask and everywhere distinguished by the beauty of their detail in doorways, windows, chimney-pieces. Never is the decoration overloaded, for the blank spaces of wall afford rest to the eye and enhance the beauty of the well-disposed detail. At Osterley Park in Middlesex, however, which dates from a few years later, Adam's weakness for over-decoration becomes first manifest. The walls are so covered with intricate Grecian detail and Etruscan stencilling that in few of the rooms is it possible even to hang a picture save in the spaces reserved for the purpose in the general scheme.

The vogue for the Adam style was intense while the architect lived; but only a few years after his death his graceful designs began to be denounced as sugary and effeminate, while even at the period of his greatest popularity there was an occasional dissentient voice. Horace Walpole, for example, wrote in 1785 of Holland's work at Carlton House: "How sick one will be after this chaste palace, of Mr. Adam's gingerbread and sippets of embroidery"; while Dr. Samuel Johnson, inspecting Kedleston with a severe eye for its defects rather than its beauties, decided that "it would do excellently for a town hall. The large room with the pillars would do for the judges to sit in at the assizes, the Circular room for a Jury chamber, and the room above for prisoners." In his diary he wrote: "The Bedchambers were small, low, dark and fitter for a prison than a house of splendour. The kitchen has openings into the gallery by which its heat and fumes are dispersed over the house." There is probably some truth in these contentions, but it must be remembered that Adam was compelled to accept the main lines of Paine's plan.

While the Adam Brothers were working on their own distinctive lines, there remained several notable exponents of stricter Palladianism such as George Dance, the architect of the Mansion House and his son (also George) who designed the splendidly virile Newgate Jail; Robert Morris, who built White Lodge in Richmond Park and the Palladian Bridge at Wilton (126); and Sir William Chambers, who altered the whole conception of bureaucratic building with his New Somerset House and designed the delightful Chinese buildings at Kew. Henry Holland, with his great Whig connection, was the only serious rival to the Adam Brothers in the domestic field, the architect of Brooks's, Southill in Bedfordshire the remodelled Althorp (102) and, finally, of Carlton House, whose somewhat *Directoire* magnificence can be studied in the colour-plate books of the close of the century.

Italy being more easily accessible to visiting architects and antiquaries, it was inevitably the Roman style that enjoyed the first flush of popularity in the ever more intensive cult of the antique. By the end of the century, however, the claims of Ancient Greece were beginning to find increasing recognition. Almost first in the field had been "Athenian" Stuart, who, with Nicholas Revett, had published *The Antiquities of Athens* as long ago as 1762; and "Grecian Gusto" had received fresh stimulus from the arrival in this country in 1801 of the famous "Elgin Marbles". While maintaining its popularity side by side with the revived Gothic until well into the middle of the next century, the Grecian manner seldom attained to the heights of achievement of its Roman predecessor, for the changing spirit of the times applied it more consistently to urban and villa building (for which it was admirably suited) than to the creation of large country houses, for which the new Gothic was gaining rapid favour. Its increasing literalism simplified internal decoration to the barest essentials, and the new rooms were left largely to rely for effect on the costliness of their window draperies and the appropriateness of their mahogany furniture, which repeated many of the forms of French Empire.

Few great names emerge at the close of the eighteenth century beyond that of Sir John Soane, whose use of the classic repertoire was so intensely individual as to make his rather rare buildings unmistakable. While his most famous work was his great reconstruction of the Bank of England, some delightful examples of his domestic style survive, such as little Pitzhanger Manor, now a municipal library, at Ealing, and Moggerhanger, Bedfordshire, now a sanatorium, and Tyringham (108), in Buckinghamshire, the latter now improved by the addition of a dome. A busier and more intrusive figure was that of John Nash, whose real talent was best expressed (to those who can remember it) in such schemes as the old Regent Street and the luckily still extant terraces of Regent's Park. Nash's devotion to stucco was derided in contemporary verse:

"Augustus at Rome was for building renown'd,
For of marble he left what of brick he had found;
But is not our Nash, too, a very great master?
He finds us all brick and he leaves us all plaster." . . .

Nevertheless, providing that it is furnished with a timely lick of paint, there is much to be said for stucco as an urban finish. The lemon-coloured squares of Bayswater and Blooms-bury, with their flounces of fresh green, have a real beauty in the early summer sunlight, while few more habitable buildings have been conceived than the middle-class villas of this period, with their striped "Trafalgar balconies", of which Rougemont House in Exeter, here illustrated (106), is a pleasant example. Nash, Decimus Burton and their con-temporaries, if their influence is hardly apparent in the evolution of the country house, left a real legacy to the spas and seaside towns, which their buildings do so much to dignify.

Beyond these solid productions, fashionable taste was hesitating on the threshold of one of its most eclectic phases. Novelty was the rage, and architects were competing with one another in a new ingenuity of domestic invention. The forces that led to the almost universal adoption of the revived Gothic in this country will be dealt with by themselves a little later, but before passing on we may well stop to cull a few of the more exotic flowers from the Regency garden to add their curious tones to the catholicity of our bouquet. There was Thomas Hope of Deepdene, for instance, a somewhat dis-agreeable amateur with a passion for furniture design, whose great wealth allowed him full scope for the realisation of his gaunt and literal interpretations of the Roman, Grecian and Egyptian styles. There was John Foulston, who rather specialised in the latter, though he could design you a house for the asking in any style from the Hindu to the Gothic. Such eclecticisms were stimulated by the almost legendary splendours of the Prince Regent's Pavilion at Brighton which, at the hands of Nash, was slowly achieving its present remarkable form (109). Here there were no false scruples as to literalism; though the swelling domes came straight from India and the dragons and lacquer panels from China, there

M

was also a touch of Saracenic and more than a touch of Gothic. But as a monument of fantasy it has never been equalled in this island; beside it the Hindu Sizencote, built for a rich Nabob in the pastoral part of Gloucestershire, appears a poor palace indeed.

Another insistent cult was that of rural simplicity, one of the earliest of its exponents being John Plaw, who at the close of the eighteenth century produced several volumes of designs for "Rural Architecture" which covered every sort of building from "the Simple Cottage to the Decorated Villa, some of which," he proudly adds, "have been executed". His edition of 1794, an interesting product of contemporary taste, opens with a frontispiece designed by the author which represents "Taste accompanying Rural Simplicity, and pointing to one of the most beautiful scenes this country can boast of, viz. The Lake of Winandermere, on the largest island in which is built a circular Villa after a design of the author's". Plaw's designs, though still principally in a thin classical style and probably intended for a stucco finish, were intensely romantic in feeling and included such obscure rustic fantasies as "Hermitages", "Shooting Farms" and a "Casine calculated for a Connoisseur". He was followed by a string of facile imitators who often carried his ideas to preposterous extremes, such as Loudon, P. F. Robinson and J. B. Papworth, the architect of Cheltenham, who in his *Rural Residences* was probably the first to coin the delicious term *cottage orné*.

The most admired plan for the great houses of the eighteenth century was that of a central block connected by curving passages to either two or four pavilions, which contained the stables, kitchens and occasionally a chapel; while sometimes one of the pavilions formed a complete house in itself which could be inhabited by the family when there were no guests to entertain, such as exists at Kedleston. At Holkham (98), where the connecting arms are short and straight, two of the pavilions contain reception rooms, and are so placed that from the end windows a vista can be obtained along the connecting arms and through the main block to the corresponding pavilion on the far side—a distance of 344 feet. The inconveniences of this type of plan, in which the kitchen might be several minutes' walk from the dining-room, are very apparent, though they were accepted quite cheerfully at the period. Mrs. Lybbe Powys, visiting the barely completed Holkham in 1756, was enchanted by its grandeur and con-

101   TRAFALGAR, WILTSHIRE.   This mid-18th Century House was presented by the Nation to the heirs of Lord Nelson

102   ALTHORP, NORTHAMPTONSHIRE, FROM THE WEST, as remodelled by
Henry Holland in 1787

venience. "Such an amazing large and good kitchen I never saw", she wrote, "everything in it so nice and clever." The owners apparently took a great interest in the domestic arrangements: "Lady Leicester . . . never misses going round this wing every morning, and one day her ladyship was seen in her kitchen at 6 o'clock (a.m.) thinking all her guests safe in bed."

It was unusual indeed to find, in a vast house of this period, the lady maintaining as personal an interest in the domestic arrangements of the establishment as her ancestors had done

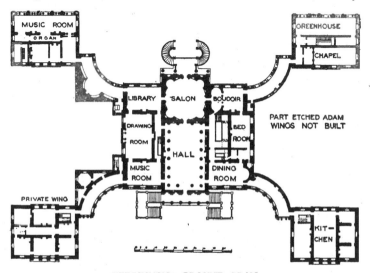

KEDLESTON : GROUND PLAN

before her in the Middle Ages. At Holkham this interest was not confined to the kitchen but also extended to the dairy, which was "the neatest place you can imagine, the whole marble". This office indeed was beginning to hold something of the allure that it exercised over the France of Marie Antoinette, and many great English houses were equipped with dairies in the most exquisite taste. Prince Pückler-Muskau, who travelled through England in 1828, observed that

> "the dairy is one of the principal decorations of an English park, and stands by itself, quite away from the cowhouse. It is generally an elegant pavilion, adorned with fountains, marble walls, and rare and beautiful porcelain, and its vessels large and small, filled with the most exquisite milk and its products, in all their varieties."

At Woburn the dairy was the central feature of a Chinese garden, and was designed like a

> "Chinese temple, decorated with a profusion of white marble and coloured glasses; in the centre is a fountain, and round the walls hundreds of large dishes and bowls of Chinese and Japan porcelain of every form and colour."

In the interior of houses built by Adam and his contemporaries, panelling and tapestry were usually discarded (though Osterley Park in Middlesex is an exception, where some of the finest rooms were built as an architectural setting for the magnificent Gobelins). The walls were now generally simple expanses of stucco painted some pale colour—pea-green, lilac or light blue—decorated by delicate plaster plaques and swags picked out in contrasting shades, with gilded detail (92). Italian or French craftsmen were sometimes brought over to execute this plasterwork, with the result that the gayest Rococo fantasies are sometimes found decorating otherwise rather restrained interiors. The detail of cornices and chimney-pieces became lighter and more fanciful, while ceilings, like walls, were enriched with plaster swags and wreaths in low relief encircling painted panels and roundels by such artists as Biagio Rebecca, Zucchi or Angelica Kauffmann. Doors were made of mahogany of the finest quality, the six panels generally outlined by a flat molding; and the greatest attention was paid to their brass furniture, which was sometimes of the utmost delicacy. In some larger houses designed by Adam the latter even incorporated some motives of the ceiling decoration.

Ornamental ironwork made a rather belated appearance in English domestic architecture. Probably the earliest example of its use had been the iron balconies on the north front of Kirby Hall, said to have been designed by Inigo Jones in 1640; but not until the arrival in this country, towards the end of the century, of an exquisite craftsman, Jean Tijou, a Huguenot refugee from France, did it come to be at all well designed or widely used. During the eighteenth century, however, it grew popular for stair balustrades and balconies, as the century advanced the designs becoming thinner and simpler. The rich robust work of Tijou, as at Chatsworth and Hampton Court, gave way to the thin elegancies of the Adam school, followed by the coarser Greek taste of the Regency. The earlier Gothic Revival had little use for ironwork, though occasional examples are to be found, such as the iron handrail

THE CULT OF THE ANTIQUE 81

of the two staircases at the Brighton Pavilion, where the metal, simulating bamboo, is twisted into a Gothic pattern.

As the nineteenth century wore on a new use was found for iron; it could be cheaply and conveniently cast into all sorts of shapes to produce the effect of the most elaborate Gothic carving. Tracery, ornaments, moldings, filigree—nothing was beyond the art of the ironfounder; and the result was more durable and, so it was felt, in almost every way superior to the original work in stone. This decoration by the yard had a wide and ready sale. But with the appearance of Ruskin its use became somewhat controversial. Was it right that, as at Eaton Hall, these clustering columns, these richly traceried windows should be cast in iron? Could this be said to be "the right use of material"? Ruskin was deeply exercised, and only after considerable deliberation was he able to reach a decision. "Iron could be used as a cement but not as a support", he announced, or, more concisely, as a tie but not as a strut.

As has been observed, the architects of the eighteenth century usually designed the greater part of the furniture for the houses they built. None were more successful in this sphere than Kent and Adam. The gilt Italianate furniture of the former, stiff and monumental though it may be, has real effectiveness in its proper setting, which is the rooms for which it was made. That of the latter shows a wider range of invention. Adam's designs vary from the riotous gilt sofas at Kedleston, decorated with dolphins and mermaids, and the great bed in the same house with posts in the form of palm-trees, to the gilded delicacies of the furniture more usually connected with his name, as at Harewood and Sion. But the majority of architects were less versatile, and there must have been a wide demand at this time for Thomas Chippendale's *Gentleman and Cabinet-maker's Director*, published in 1752, which provided somewhat similar assistance to the country carpenter as Batty Langley's books did to the builder —though in this case the author was also an extremely successful practitioner of the art on which he wrote. Although others published books on the same subject, none was so thorough, none covered so wide a field as Chippendale's. Designed to assist "Persons in all degrees of Life", his book contained drawings for pieces of every kind, and in the two later editions, examples in different styles including the Gothic and the fashionable Chinese. Chippendale's exact status as a designer has been assailed, but if the splendid furniture

usually credited to him is indeed his work he was an artist
of the first rank.

Soon, however, the cabriole legs, flowing ribbons and
rococo detail of his school came to be abandoned for the
square tapered legs and simple lines advocated by Thomas
Sheraton (1751–1806), whose sanction of ornament of any
kind was generally at first confined to a discreet use of
marquetry. But towards the end of his career, as taste became
increasingly influenced by the French Empire style, his maxim
that decoration should be strictly subservient to construction
was considerably relaxed, and can hardly be said to apply at all
to his final productions. After his death the Empire influence
grew more literal, though there is often a homeliness and
grace in the English mahogany of the Regency period that
is lacking in its Napoleonic counterparts.

The latter half of the eighteenth century was a period of
widespread wealth and social activity. The vast size of the
rooms of the new country houses demanded a perpetual
concourse of visitors, and parties for music, cards or dancing
were indulged in as actively in the country as in London or
Bath, the guests risking the many discomforts and dangers
of long drives over rough roads for the pleasures of these
tonish gatherings. Mrs. Lybbe Powys, most enthusiastic of
party-goers, has left descriptions of several of these occasions
so graphic that they are worth quoting *in extenso*. To begin
with there is a little open-air gathering near Chesterfield
during the summer of 1757, while the authoress was still the
blushing and immature Miss Girle:

> "The gardens are charming, and as we drank tea in one of the
> buildings, the family being very musical, the young ladies
> sang, while the gentlemen accompanied on their German
> flutes. This little concert took up the heat of the day, after
> which we walk'd over the grounds. When in a little temple,
> on entering we laughed exceedingly at the rural politeness
> of our beaux; but as gentlemen of the army are always gallant,
> we were less surprised at our elegant collation of fruits, cakes,
> cream, placed in the most neat and rustic manner imaginable."

A more elaborate entertainment was that given at Fawley
Court near Henley some ten years later. The account provides
an interesting description of the reception rooms.

> "Their usual eating room not being large enough, the supper
> was in the hall, so that we did not come in thro' that, but a

103 WARDOUR CASTLE, WILTSHIRE (1776). By James Paine. Notice the austerity of the " Landscape " Lay-out

104 HEVENINGHAM HALL, SUFFOLK: the Dining-room.
Redecorated by James Wyatt in 1790

105 THE OLD RECTORY, HUSBORNE CRAWLEY, BEDFORDSHIRE:
Decoration and Furniture of *circa* 1800

window was taken out of the library, and a temporary flight
of steps made into that, from which we passed into the green
breakfast-room (that night the tea-room); thro' the pink
paper billiard-room, along the saloon, into the red damask
drawing room. Though none set down, this room was soon
so crowded as to make us return to the saloon. This likewise
very soon fill'd, and as the tea was carrying round, one heard
from every one, 'Fine assembly,' 'Magnificent house,' 'Sure
we are in London.' They danced in the Saloon, no minuets
that night, they would have been difficult without a master
of the ceremonies among so many people of rank. Two
card-rooms, the drawing-room and eating-room. The latter
looking so elegant lighted up; two tables at Loo, one quinze,
one vingt-une, many whist."

The play was rather high and Mrs. Powys prudently
declined to join a table. "Oh what a disfiguring thing is
gaming," she exclaims, "especially for ladies!" The party
continued for many hours.

"The orgeat, lemonade, capillaire, and red and white negus,
with cakes, were carried round the whole evening. At half
an hour after twelve the supper was announced, and the hall
doors thrown open, on entering which nothing could be
more striking, as you know 'tis so fine a one, and was then
illuminated by three hundred colour'd lamps round the six
doors, over the chimney, and over the statue at the other end.
The tables had a most pleasing effect, ornamented with everything in the confectionery way, and festoons and wreaths
of artificial flowers prettily disposed; all fruits of the season,
as grapes, pines, etc.; fine wines, everything conducted with
great ease—no bustle. Ninety-two sat down to supper. . . .
After supper they returned to dancing, chiefly then cotillons,
till near six."

Picnics were another popular form of entertainment and
Mrs. Powys describes a party of this nature in the romantic
Forest of Needwood, which was attended by the usual
inconveniences :—

"Mr and Mrs Bailey had drove early in the morning to the
Forest, to see all the dining-tables placed under the shade of
the trees; and a most elegant cold collation indeed it was,
or at least I may say intended to be so, but we none of us
could help laughing with the donors themselves, who told
us, in placing the tables in the most shady parts, they had
litterally forgotten the sun was drawing on to that spot, as

well as their visitors, so that the intense heat of the weather made the hams, tongues, chickens, pies etc., etc., litterally all lukewarm."

But the musical party was modish beyond all others; whether it entailed listening to "two famous musicians, the Leaders, play on the French horn" or to little Miss Randal, aged six years, who "plays on the piano in a most wonderful manner, and has a sweet voice; she is accompanied on the harp by her blind father and her uncle, Mr. Parry, on the flageolet"; or attending a vast concert given by "the amiable Lady Nelson," when music was performed "supposed to be expressive of her lord's victories". "The Battle of the Nile," unfortunately, "was only a monstrous continued noise." "But," Mrs. Powys kindly adds, "everyone was grateful to her ladyship."

So the time passed very agreeably for these Georgian ladies whose stately movements almost come to life in the more domestic canvases of Zoffany and the earlier Gainsborough. The country house formed an ideal background for their leisurely gossiping lives in which the prime activities would seem to have been the bearing of children and attending of parties.

During the last years of the eighteenth century meals became of a much more elaborate nature, so much so that the dinner menu was now often arranged in two services, each of which was a complete repast in itself. A dinner given in honour of Prince William of Gloucester in 1798 furnishes a good example. It consisted of:—

Salmon Trout

Soles

Fricando of Veal.   Rais'd Giblet Pie.

Vegetable Pudding.

Chickens.   Ham.

Muffin Pudding.

Curry of Rabbits.   Preserve of Olives.

Soup.   Haunch of Venison.

Open Tart Syllabub.   Rais'd Jelly.

Three Sweetbreads, larded.

Maccaroni.   Buttered Lobster.

Peas.

Potatoes.

Baskets of Pastry.   Custards.

Goose.

106 ROUGEMONT HOUSE, EXETER : Bow-windows and Trafalgar
Balconies of *circa* 1810

107 BROADLANDS, HAMPSHIRE : the Hall, showing a typical
Sculpture Display of the Regency Period

108 TYRINGHAM, BUCKINGHAMSHIRE: the Entrance Front. Sir John Soane, Architect, *circa* 1796. The Dome was added in 1907-8 from a design founded on Bagatelle

109 THE ROYAL PAVILION, BRIGHTON. Built for the Prince Regent by John Nash, and completed in 1827. A Night View

The sequence of the courses seems rather arbitrary, but it must be remembered that the majority of the dishes were placed upon the table, so that the guests could help themselves in whichever order they pleased. A dinner cooked by the celebrated chef Carême for the Prince Regent at the Brighton Pavilion was lately repeated in this more abstemious age; but although consisting of upwards of twenty courses accompanied by an equal number of different wines, its consumption did not prove an impossible task for twentieth-century stomachs.

Long and elaborate dinners were not solely a royal prerogative. "A party of seventeen—a most superb dinner, eighteen dishes the first course, including the two soups" was a not unusual event. No trouble was too great to produce the perfect meal, and in 1804, when George III, in one of his more lucid intervals, visited Culham Court near Wycombe, the anxious host "had hot rolls brought from Gunter, wrapped in flannel, by relays of horsemen". Fortunately the King appreciated the attention and remarked "Ah, Gunter, Gunter! I am glad you deal with Gunter. Nobody like Gunter!" His Majesty insisted on dining at one o'clock, which was not at this period at all the usual hour. In 1757 breakfast had been at eight, dinner at two; half a century later, however, dinner was commonly eaten at four and supper at half past nine.

The service of meals was such a commonplace that there is little mention of it in contemporary English memoirs; it is to Prince Pückler-Muskau, most observant of recorders, that we owe the minute description of an English dinner in 1826:—

"The gentlemen lead the ladies into the dining room, not as in France, by the hand, but by the arm. When you enter, you find the whole of the first course on the table, as in France. After the soup is removed, and the covers are taken off, every man helps the dish before him, and offers some of it to his neighbour; if he wishes for anything else, he must ask across the table, or send a servant for it; a very troublesome custom, in place of which, some of the most elegant travelled gentlemen have adopted the more convenient German fashion of sending the servants round with the dishes. . . . It is not usual to take wine without drinking to another person. If the company is small, and a man has drunk with everybody, but happens to wish for more wine, he must wait for the desert, if he does not find in himself courage enough to brave custom. . . . At the conclusion of the second course comes a sort of intermediate dessert of cheese, butter, salad, raw

N

celery, and the like; after which ale sometimes thirty or
forty years old, and so strong that when thrown on the fire
it blazes like a spirit, is handed about. The table-cloth is then
removed: under it, at the best tables, is a finer, upon which
the dessert is set. At inferior ones, it is placed on the bare
polished table. It consists of all sorts of hot-house fruits,
which are here of the finest quality, Indian and native pre-
serves, stomachic ginger, confitures and the like. Clean glasses
are set before every guest, and, with the dessert plates and
knives and forks, small fringed napkins are laid. Three
decanters are usually placed before the master of the house,
generally containing claret, port, sherry or madeira. The host
pushes these on stands, or in a little silver waggon on wheels,
to his neighbour on the left. The ladies sit a quarter of an
hour longer, during which time sweet wines are sometimes
served, and then rise from table."

It is difficult to discover the exact point at which the wave
of Romantic feeling that was to lead to the revival of Gothic
architecture first made itself felt in this country. It must be
remembered that the old tradition of Gothic building had
died hard in country districts, maintaining a flicker of life
in the village architecture of the Cotswolds and other remote
parts of the kingdom until well after the Restoration. Its
demise almost synchronised with the newly whetted interest
of such rarefied spirits as Horace Walpole and Gray, whose
first Romantic hankerings were anticipating the impulses of
a generation or more later, when the spark had been fanned
to a flame by the doctrines of Rousseau and the upheavals
of the French Revolution.

The first feeling for the "natural" was, rightly one feels,
chiefly applied to gardens and parks. "Capability" Brown and,
later, Humphrey Repton, ordained that the immediate surroundings of the classical mansions of the eighteenth century
should not be marred by an obtrusive formality; although the
architecture might be Italian, there was to be no nonsense
of Italian gardens. Petty detail was to be eliminated; the
expanses of the park were to sweep to the very windows (103),
while so vulgar a necessity as a kitchen garden was to be
banished to a distance of half a mile or more and there concealed by a grove of trees. In some cases, so that the house
might be surrounded by sward on every side, the back premises
were approached by an under-ground passage down which
the staff and tradesmen could disappear like rabbits at a
discreet distance. An alternative method was adopted at

110 SPEKE HALL, LANCASHIRE: the Entrance
From a Water Colour by Joseph Nash, Author of *Mansions of England in the Olden Time*

Harleyford near Marlow, where "the whole of the offices were so contriv'd in a pit, as to be perfectly invisible. A great addition", the description continues, "to the look of any place, and certainly adds infinitely to the neatness so conspicuous round Harleyford." The almost certain discomfort and inconvenience of offices so arranged was not considered.

Following the lead given by a handful of *dilettanti*, it soon began to be felt by persons of taste that the classical manner was hardly consonant with "natural" and "romantic" yearnings. So blatantly the outcome of mathematical rule, it was hardly a fitting accompaniment to the studied carelessness of groves and lakes. There was little link, for instance, between Kedleston and nature. The Gothic ruin had long been an object of romantic interest as viewed through the classical sash window, but how far better to admire it through a Gothic casement.

Professional architects were quick as ever to adapt their talents to the new taste; Mr. James Wyatt, for instance, most versatile of men, was equally ready to design a house in style of a Roman palace or of a Tudor monastery. Of course there had been numerous exponents of Gothic before his time; indeed few architects of repute had refrained from trying their hand, usually with disastrous results, at something in the "Gothick taste". Batty Langley, among his twenty-odd helpful volumes, had devoted more than one to this romantic art; Wren had sought to employ the style in the building of Tom Tower at Christ Church, Oxford; Hawksmoor in 1735 had added the "Gothic" towers to the west end of Westminster Abbey. In 1754 Millar had designed a flamboyant Gothic archway at Lacock, and about 1760 Robert Adam a rather thin church at Croome in Worcestershire. But ten years before this last date Horace Walpole was already adding to and embellishing his cottage at Strawberry Hill, not only employing Gothic detail on the exterior but giving to the interiors what he considered a genuine medieval finish. Where rooms were added these were no mere drawing-rooms and dining-rooms, but Galleries and Refectories.

After the turn of the century the public interest in the Gothic Revival was tremendously stimulated by the flood of Romantic novels which Sir Walter Scott poured forth from battlemented Abbotsford; and though Eastlake doubted whether the novelist "possessed anything more than a superficial knowledge of the art he so enthusiastically admired", there can be no doubt that his writings exercised a stronger influence than any number of textbooks. The latter, however, were not wanting for the student embued with an enthusiasm for the Christian style, and the indefatigable Augustus Pugin, a fugitive of the French Revolution and Nash's principal perspective draughtsman, was able to employ the greater part of a profitable career in the compilation of such works as *The Specimens* and *Examples of Gothic Architecture*, which remain fruitful sources for the study of medieval detail. A later flower of the public enthusiasm for Plantagenet England was Joseph Nash's *Mansions of England in the Olden Time*, which began to appear in lithographic plates during the later 'thirties. Houses were here portrayed as nearly as possible in their original state in those merry times when, again to quote Eastlake,

> "there was feasting in the hall and tilting in the courtyard, when the yule log crackled on the hearth, and mummers beguiled the dulness of a winter's evening, when the bowling green was filled with lusty youths, and gentle dames sat spinning in their boudoirs, when the deep window recesses were filled with family groups, and gallant cavaliers rode out a-hawking. . . ."

But Nash's plates speak for themselves.

James Wyatt (1746–1813) was, then, the first practical exponent on a large scale of revived Gothic in this country. In 1787 he had carried out the renovations and alterations to Salisbury Cathedral that had earned him the unenviable epithet of "The Destroyer", and which would appear to have stimulated in him an enthusiasm for Gothic that was to find sensational later expression in those mammoth and fantastic palaces of Fonthill and Ashridge. Although his Gothic essays were ripe with medieval detail, his planning, as appears most emphatically at Ashridge, remained conventionally symmetrical and classic; but it would have been considered a heresy at the time to admit, as must be admitted now, that his buildings in the Greco-Italian manner, such as Heaton Park at Manchester, are far superior, for all their array of spires and pinnacles, to anything he attempted in Gothic.

The circumstances of the rise and fall of Fonthill Abbey were so remarkable, and fit so superbly into the early romantic phases of the Gothic Revival, that they may well be described, however briefly, in detail. Beckford, the attractive and capricious heir to the greatest fortune in England, largely derived from plantations in the West Indies, decided on his majority in 1780 to encircle the greater part of his Wiltshire estate by a wall 12 feet high to ensure that no follower of the Chase, which he abhorred, should encroach upon his lands. A mansion thus secluded within so insurmountable a barricade quickly became an object of mystery and interest—an interest that was whetted by the accounts of strange doings within the house and the curious genius that streaked every page of its master's literary productions. The curiosity spread beyond Wiltshire when work was started on the new Gothic "Abbey". So intense indeed did it become that a local peer, overcome by his desire for first-hand knowledge, procured a ladder and scaled the wall. He was detected and brought to Beckford, who treated his noble trespasser with extreme courtesy, showing him all he wished to see and finally dismissing him with every mark of esteem. As he attempted to depart, however, his lordship found every gate locked against him and had perforce to leave the domain as he had entered it, by a ladder.

Beckford's first intention had been merely to decorate his park with the ruin of a Gothic convent, which latter was erected in 1796 from the designs of James Wyatt. Ten years later, however, he decided to abandon the classical mansion of his father, which he had always disliked, and enlarge the ruin for his actual habitation. The finished result was on a scale far beyond anything contemplated in the first enthusiasm. Beckford's building mania left him the possessor of an immense cruciform structure, 312 by 250 feet in its main dimensions, surmounted at the crossing by a tower that rose 278 feet into the astonished air of Wiltshire. The principal feature of the interior was a hall 78 feet high, decorated with the armorial bearings of the great families connected by marriage with that of Beckford, at the far end of which a long flight of steps rose through a soaring Gothic arch to the saloon beneath the tower. In addition there were dining-rooms, libraries, oratories, cloisters and "cortiles", all decorated with the richest Gothic detail culled by Mr. Wyatt from a wide variety of original sources; the entrance gateway was copied from St. Augustine's Abbey at Canterbury, the windows of the saloon from the Royal Monastery at Batalha, and so on. The interior was magnificently fitted up, and housed the famous collection of *objets d'arts* brought together by the owner.

So great was Beckford's impatience to complete his abbey

that the work of construction was continued both day and night, nearly 500 employees continuing in shifts, lighted at night by flares, so that the building might be made habitable in record time. This undue haste proved its downfall, as the contractor was thereby enabled to omit, undetected, the inverted arches provided in the specification for the support of the tower. Beckford did not learn of this omission until after he had sold the estate and retired, with a splenetic temper and depleted income, to Bath, where he solaced his declining years by the erection of the curious Lansdowne Tower that is still a landmark. He immediately informed the new owner, who replied cheerfully that he anticipated the house would last his lifetime. His confidence, however, was misplaced, for soon after the tower collapsed in a gale. The Abbey was never repaired, and a few years later the remains were pulled down. Thus, after an existence of only quarter of a century, this fantastic palace, which had cost over £273,000 to build, had entirely vanished.

Ashridge (111) was still incomplete on Wyatt's death in a carriage accident in 1813, but the work was carried on by his nephew, Jeffry Wyatt, better known to posterity as Sir Jeffry Wyattville. The latter's talents were never entirely devoted to Gothic, however, for he had made vast additions to Chatsworth in a thin Italian manner, and alterations to Longleat in an unfortunately more robust version of the Early Renaissance style. But it is for his transformations at Windsor that he is principally famous. That improvements were necessary is clear from a description of the deplorable state of the Castle in 1766. "The furniture is old and dirty, most of the best pictures removed to the Queen's palace, and the whole kept so very un-neat that it hurts one to see almost the only place in England worthy to be styled our King's Palace so totally neglected." Winning a competition against Nash and Smirke in 1824, Wyattville spent, during the following years, over half a million pounds for his royal patron. Although his Gothic detail is coarse and crude in the extreme, he converted the Castle from an almost uninhabitable rabbit-warren of rooms into a building of great grandeur and, for a royal palace, of some convenience; while by heightening the Round Tower and judiciously pruning the others, he gave this amorphous group of buildings a romance and beauty of outline which it had never previously possessed.

Pückler-Muskau, who visited the castle in 1827 while still in course of reconstruction, considered it "already the vastest and most magnificent residence possessed by any sovereign in Europe". The grateful monarch conferred a knighthood on the architect, and allowed him to pander to his rather childish feeling for the medieval and romantic by giving his surname its Norman-sounding suffix, and adding to his coat-of-arms a view of the George IV gateway at Windsor. It may be mentioned that the desire to give an ordinary English name a more blue-blooded flavour was not rare at this period; there are many examples among the peerages conferred by George III and George IV of these "sham antiques". Mr. Maude, for example, became Baron de Montalt, Mr. French, Baron de Freyne and Mr. Basset, Baron de Dunstanville, while medieval enthusiasts who were not fortunate enough to acquire peerages simply changed their names by licence. Green became de Freville; Wilkins, de Winton; Gossop, de Rodes; Hunt, de Vere; Mullins, de Moleyns; Morres, de Montmorency, to give only a few instances. In this new plumage the owners of Gothic Revival castles no doubt considered themselves the equals in feudal dignity of their Plantagenet predecessors, even though their incomes were derived from extensive coal interests or their activity in the enclosure of their tenants' commons.

Wyatt and Wyattville were undoubtedly the most considerable figures of the earlier Gothic Revival, but both these technically talented exponents give the impression of having been mentally too near the classicism of the eighteenth century to enter more than superficially into the spirit of the medieval style. The same may be said of Sir Charles Barry, whose early Gothic experiment at Toddington Manor (*circa* 1830), here illustrated (112), makes an interesting comparison with his later achievement at the Palace of Westminster. The battlemented pediment, as may be seen at Hartland Abbey in Devon, a favourite if paradoxical part of the repertoire of the first Revival architects, was not, one feels, even to these men an impossibility.

The increasing literalism that distinguished most of the later productions of the revival was largely a result of the activities of the Pugin family. The first of this line, Charles Augustus (1762–1832), had, as had been seen, immensely stimulated Gothic production by his published collections of detail. It remained for his son, Augustus Welby Northmore (1819–1852), by his profuse and fiery writings as by his singularly eccentric example, to make the first serious attempt at a reversion to the basic principles of medieval building—

for, as a fervent convert to Catholicism, he felt that Gothic was the only truly "Christian architecture", and set down his belief with a pictorial and literary emphasis that are almost sad to study to-day. It was at this period that a rich Catholic nobleman, the Earl of Shrewsbury, was indulging his extravagant passion for building by the erection of a mammoth house in the most romantic Gothic manner at Alton in Staffordshire. More robust in style than Ashridge, more spiritual in feeling than Fonthill, the dining-hall was copied from the Sainte Chapelle in Paris while the entrance hall resembled the nave of some debased cathedral. Another room was built in the form of an octagonal chapter-house, the stucco tracery of the roof springing from a central clustered shaft, while the romantic atmosphere was enhanced by a variety of full-length plaster tombs disposed around the walls. This remarkable house had already assumed gigantic proportions when the second Pugin attracted its owner's attention, and was engaged to make elaborate additions to the fantastic but fascinating pile. These additions, though not particularly attractive in themselves, show a knowledge and understanding of Gothic far in advance of their time, and are in striking contrast to the carefree earlier work produced between 1809 and 1823.

A. W. Pugin, though considered a revolutionary in his time, really ushered in the second and heavier phase of the Gothic Revival, the phase of Scott and Street and Waterhouse, of the conscientious despoliation of some of our loveliest cathedrals and churches in the sacred cause of "restoration", and the burgeoning of a staggering crop of Gothic town-halls, art galleries and termini in London and the provincial cities. It is here that we must leave the country house to a phase of lavish and heavy-handed mediocrity of which Waterhouse's Eaton Hall in Cheshire is a fairly conspicuous example. It was a phase that was not to last for long, for a new generation, stimulated by the doctrines of Ruskin and William Morris, was soon to bring a welcome breath of inspiration into the stagnant atmosphere of English domestic architecture, and place its productions far ahead of those of other countries. The work of Norman Shaw and Philip Webb was continued by such talented innovators as Ernest Newton and C. F. A. Voysey, while more recently Sir Edwin Lutyens, in the numerous houses that his lively talent has scattered about the English countryside, has shown himself at least the master of a variety of styles and materials.

111 ASHRIDGE PARK, HERTFORDSHIRE : the South Front. Designed by James Wyatt in 1806 and completed by his nephew, Wyattville

112 TODDINGTON MANOR, GLOUCESTERSHIRE : the South Terrace. Built by Sir Charles Barry in 1829

113 TODDINGTON MANOR, GLOUCESTERSHIRE (1829): the Library.
An early Essay by Sir Charles Barry in his Houses of Parliament manner

114 HUGHENDEN MANOR, BUCKINGHAMSHIRE: Disraeli's
Drawing-room. Early Victorian Decoration at its best

115 LONGFORD CASTLE, WILTSHIRE: the Parterre, with the South Front as rebuilt by

CHAPTER V

THE GARDEN

UNTIL the fifteenth century the possession of a garden was chiefly confined to monasteries, but with the building of domestic manor-houses it became an essential appendage. At first it was of the simplest and most utilitarian nature—consisting of a moderate-sized square or circular enclosure surrounded, when possible, by a wall or, failing so stout a protection, by a wattle fence or thorn hedge. The size was very restricted, and so continued until well into the following century; but the smallest area must have sufficed for the limited number of herbs which were grown, while the cultivation of vegetables was almost entirely neglected.

This appears clearly in Holinshed's *Chronicle* of 1580:

> "Such herbs, roots and fruits as grow yearly out of the ground have been very plentiful in the time of the first Edward and after his days; but in the process of time they also grew to be neglected, so that from Henry IV until the latter end of Henry VII and the beginning of Henry VIII there was little or no use of them in England, but they remained either unknown or supposed as food more meet for hogs and savage beasts than mankind."

The English apparently held the same opinion of all vegetables as the French hold to-day of the Broad Bean.

Only by monks were vegetables continuously cultivated, for the sound reason that to some Orders, such as the Benedictines who at first eat no meat, the produce of the garden was an essential addition to a diet which would otherwise have consisted entirely of fish from the ponds.

The medieval manor-house garden, therefore, was principally given over to herbs, and the few flowers which were grown were tolerated rather for their flavouring value than for their beauty. Violets, daisies and columbines were good for soup; primrose buds, daisies, red fennel and the violet for salads, while the latter flower, with the addition of sorel and mint, was much used for sauces. The only ornamental feature in an early garden was a raised earth mound covered with turf which was used as a seat.

Fruit trees were plentiful, but were grown outside the herb

garden in order not to keep the light from the sun-loving plants. Most of the simpler varieties of fruits were cultivated such as apples, pears, cherries, medlars and mulberries.

An early description of an English garden occurs in the verses written by James I of Scotland while imprisoned in Windsor Castle from 1406–1423:

"Now was there made, fast by the Towris wall,
A garden fair;—and in the corners set
An arbour green, with wandis long and small
Railed about, and so with trees set
Was all the place, and Hawthorne hedges knet . . ."

The verses following describe more arbours and alleys, and "the sharpe greene sweet Juniper", and these must have been the principal features of pleasure gardens. There is no mention of any flowers. Sometimes, however, these were allowed to encroach on the Herb Garden, and the lily and the rose would be found flourishing among the rue, the sage, the basil and the mint.

Herbs were as important a feature of a medieval garden as fruit. Not only were they used for cooking, but even more extensively for the curing of every conceivable ailment. There was also an occasional Love Philter or Poison Potion to be considered, but as far as one knows no garden herbs were especially grown for the distillation of these important draughts; also, as in the earliest days gardens were mostly confined to monasteries, there can have been no very urgent demand for them. For medicinal purposes, however, a large supply of herbs was absolutely essential, as the monks acted as doctors not only to the brethren but to the inhabitants of the surrounding districts.

During the latter half of the fifteenth century a distinction became apparent between the ornamental and the purely useful herbs. The "Nosegaie Garden" contained "the herbes and flowers used to make nosegaies and garlands of", while the humbler varieties were segregated in an enclosure which soon developed into the kitchen garden. The "nosegaies and gar- lands" must have suffered from a certain sameness, as the number of different varieties of flowers was very limited: Rose, Lily, Violet, Clove-pink and Periwinkle appear to have been the only available species to choose from. The first three flowers of this short list had the additional merit of being credited with a curative effect on a variety of ills.

The flowers were sparsely grown in beds which were either

oblong parterres or raised mounds of earth, sometimes as much as a foot high, supported by boards, and ranged round the outer hedge or wattle fence of the garden.

With the sixteenth century came a great revival of interest and enterprise in gardening. Harrison complacently remarks that "the ancient gardens were but dung hills", and enlarges on the great number of plants which had been lately imported from abroad. "Many strange herbs, plants and annual fruits", he writes, "are daily brought unto us from the Indies, Americans, Taprobane, Canary Isles and all parts of the world."

Simultaneously with the importation of new plants came a considerable alteration in the structure of the garden. Until the time of the Tudors the general form and layout had been solely dictated by necessity, and little thought had been given to picturesque effect; but the Italian craftsmen brought to this country by Henry VIII did more than merely adorn the houses with classical detail; they introduced the fashion of the architectural and formal garden. At this period the raised terrace supported by a bank or wall was first introduced. From the terrace, steps would lead down to an Italian garden which would be ornamented with marble fountains and grottoes.

In the few existing pictures of Nonsuch Palace, built for himself by Henry VIII, the formal layout of the gardens can be clearly seen. Between four parterres, which are separated by paths, stand three stone ornaments, two pillars surmounted by birds, which, as described by Hentzner, "streamed water from their bills", and a grand central feature, apparently a fountain; on either side of the house appear a variety of other rather astonishing objects. The restricted resources of nature were sometimes augmented by the introduction of highly coloured wooden figures of heraldic beasts. Henry VIII, having obtained possession of Hampton Court from Wolsey, had a large number of such animals set up on the top of green and white poles in what now became "The King's Privy Garden". He also ordered 38 stone statues of Kings and Queens, a quantity of dragons, lions, greyhounds, harts, and unicorns, 16 of the "King's Beasts", and 16 sundials. The gardens, which at that period can have covered only a few acres, must have indeed teemed with ferocious shapes, and the result must have been as remote from the true Italian garden as was the highly decorated Tudor house from the Italian villa.

But the average Tudor garden was a far simpler affair, in

which statues and architectural features were unknown and the charm lay in the quiet shade of trees and arbours, so soothingly described by Spenser:

> "And all without were walkes and alleys dight
> With divers trees enrang'd in even rankes;
> And here and there were pleasant arbors pight,
> And shadie seats, and sundry flowring bankes,
> To sit and rest the walkers wearie shanks."

The Italian style of garden achieved little popularity in England until the last quarter of the sixteenth century, when the Elizabethan *nouveaux riches* were erecting their vast new houses in the flamboyant Early Renaissance style. The modest Tudor garden seemed shabby and out of place, and it became essential to lay out a new and more appropriate setting for these grandiose palaces. The walled enclosure was often retained, but the more homely fruit trees were banished out of immediate sight of the principal windows. A terrace would be raised along the front of the house, with steps descending to gravel walks which divided the former vegetable patch into equal divisions: these spaces were then transformed by little hedges of dwarf box into flower beds of intricate pattern. These knot gardens, as they were called, could assume almost any shape, and sometimes even reproduced the scroll design of the surrounding brickwork. A little height was given by the clipped trees of yew or box, and variety of tone introduced by scattering the paths between the clipped hedges with coloured sand, ashes or gravel. At the central junction of the paths there was usually some feature carved in stone, such as a sundial or a fountain. On the far side would be a raised terrace parallel to that under the house, bounded by a wall descending to the grass of the park. Such terraces had a twofold function in forming an agreeable elevated walk from which a view of house, garden and park could be obtained, and in providing an insurmountable barrier against deer or cattle.

Although at this period there was still not the vast variety of flowers that is procurable now, there was no serious lack of them, and the intricate patterned gardens could be so planted as to provide a very delightful display. Indeed, the majority of flowers which are to be seen in any simple cottage garden were also known to the Elizabethans, and only of flowering shrubs does there appear to have been an almost complete dearth.

116 BLICKLING HALL, NORFOLK (early 17th Century) : the Formal Garden

118 MONTACUTE, SOMERSET : One of the
twin Garden Pavilions of *circa* 1599

117 WILTON, WILTSHIRE : the " Holbein Porch," said to
have been designed by the Artist in the early 16th Century

Where there were no walls the gardens were divided by pleached alleys of lime, apple or pear, which formed pleasant shady walks in hot weather.

The pavilions were one of the most attractive features of an Elizabethan garden. There were usually two of these, built in the same style as, and placed in formal relation to, the house, which they thus had the effect of bringing into closer relationship with the garden. Occasionally they were divided by floors into two or more rooms, some of which had fireplaces, but more usually they consisted of a single large room. One of the prettiest pair of pavilions of this period is to be seen at Montacute in Somerset, where the garden is one of the most beautiful surviving examples of the Elizabethan layout (118), though the "knots" and paths have been replaced by simple expanses of lawn.

The unsettled years of Civil War and Commonwealth were not productive of many new ideas or improvements in garden design. When Charles II returned to England, however, after years of forced sojourn in France, he was primed with knowledge of French methods, though his resources were always too restricted to allow of many alterations to his rather derelict palaces. Nevertheless, the "grand manner" of laying out the surroundings of a house, as exemplified by Le Notre at Versailles, was gradually assimilated by English gardeners, and during the half century following the Restoration some splendid examples were produced in this country. With the coming of William of Orange, the Dutch garden became popular, and until well into the eighteenth century these two styles, French and Dutch, enjoyed a parallel popularity. For the large garden a grand layout in the style of le Notre was considered most suitable. The radiating glades and formal canals and fountains produced an effect of extreme spaciousness and dignity. But never, in this country, were gardens carried out on a scale as imposing as those at Versailles or Vaux-le-Vicomte, where a succession of pools, canals, cascades and avenues of trees carry the eye to almost infinite distances. Only at Wrest Park in Bedfordshire where the layout can, for beauty, challenge comparison with any in France (128), and at Hampton Court, where three great walks, bordered by yews, spread fanwise from the centre of the Wren façade and lead through wrought-iron gates to avenues and long canals across the park, are there outstanding examples of the Louis XIV style.

One is glad to know that the gardens at Hampton Court

P

were contemporarily admired. "The gardens were designed to be very ffine, Great fountaines and Grass plotts and grave walkes, and just against the middle of ye house was a very large fountaine, and beyond it a large Cannal Guarded by rows of Even trees that runn a good way. There was fine carving in the Iron Gates in the Gardens with all sorts of ffigures, and Iron spikes Round on a breast wall and severall Rows of trees."

The idea of the Dutch garden was very different, and had far more in common with the English Elizabethan style. The enclosure was cut up into large divisions by thick clipped hedges of yew or box or alleys of pleached limes or beech, with "windows" cut at regular intervals. Within these hedges the space was laid out in a rather similar manner to the knot garden, but the designs were more elaborate. Coloured gravels were still used to give variety to the form of the clipped box hedges. At Blenheim Palace a magnificent garden of this sort has been constructed during the last few years according to the original designs. Crushed stone and marble form patterns in pink, blue and yellow which are outlined by dwarf hedges of clipped box curling in geometrical patterns like elaborate iron work.

Topiary work became increasingly popular during the reign of William and Mary, and by the early years of the eighteenth century had reached such a fantastic pitch that *The Spectator*, that energetic critic of contemporary manners and customs, felt compelled to draw attention to what it considered a debased form of gardening:

"Our trees rise in Cones, Globes, and Pyramids. We see the Marks of the Scissors upon every Plant and Bush. I do not know whether I am singular in my Opinion, but, for my own part, I would rather look upon a Tree in all its Luxuriancy and Diffusion of Boughs and Branches, than when it is thus cut and trimmed into a Mathematical Figure."

The Guardian also poured ridicule on contemporary gardens, and published a "Catalogue of greens to be disposed of by an eminent town gardener. . . . Adam and Eve in Yew; Adam a little shattered by the fall of the Tree of Knowledge in the great storm; Eve and the Serpent very flourishing. St. George in Box; his arm scarce long enough, but will be in a Condition to stick the dragon by next April. A Green dragon of the same with a tail of ground Ivy for the present. A pair of Giants stunted, to be sold Cheap. A Quickset

119 BURTON AGNES, YORKSHIRE: the Gatehouse (*circa* 1600)

120 GUNTON PARK, NORFOLK: The Parish Church simulating a
Garden Temple (1769)

121 CHASTLETON HOUSE, OXFORDSHIRE: Topiary Work
in the Circular Rose Garden

hedge, shot up into a porcupine, by its being forgot a week in rainy weather", and so forth.

These fantasies were no doubt the product of the lively imagination of the writer, invented to give weight to his sarcasm; but that few subjects were considered beyond the scope of topiary work is clear from the specimens that have survived. In the garden at Chastleton in Oxfordshire, for example, there is a startling circle of clipped trees consisting of animals, heraldic beasts, and ships cut in yew and box which date from about 1700 (121), and, though some have had to be renewed, the original forms have been retained.

The surroundings of houses were very rigidly laid out. The approach would be through wrought-iron gates into a courtyard surrounded by a low wall surmounted by an iron *clair voyée* made up, perhaps, of "iron barres and spikes, painted blew with gold tops, and brickwork between ye gates and pillars with stone tops carv'd like flower potts". Beds and parterres, encircled by low box hedges and interspersed with topiary work and "Brass Statues Great and Small", or "dwarfe trees, both ffruites and green", were divided by broad paths leading to avenues which stretched away, if we can credit Kipp's and Badeslade's ubiquitous views, to the distant sky-line, while somewhere, concealed in a formal grove, would be a grotto or a wilderness. So few layouts on this grand scale have survived, however, that one is inclined to doubt if many of them were ever carried out at all, or were even more than an optimistic plan in the mind of the architect. But at Boughton in Northamptonshire a scheme on the most grandiose scale was definitely executed for the first Duke of Montagu, who, returning about 1680 from the court of Versailles entranced by what he had seen, hastened to make huge additions to his house in the French style, and laid out avenues and groves interspersed with statues. The scheme was subsequently enlarged by his son, and eventually stretched for miles into the prosaic landscape of Northamptonshire. But, alas, in these utilitarian days the layout has been broken up in the interests of farming, and only an occasional statue sadly surveying a ploughed field now bears witness to the extent of this ambitious conception. But that the drawings of Kip were essentially correct in the details of the formal gardens round the house can be proved from structural features which still remain. At Hamstead Marshall in Berkshire, for example, where house and garden have completely disappeared with the exception of the magni-

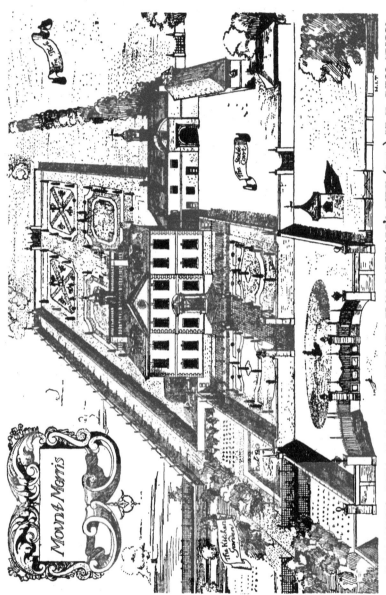

MOUNT MORRIS, KENT: THE LAYOUT REDRAWN FROM BADESLADE'S VIEW (1720) BY H. INIGO TRIGGS

ficent brick and stone gate piers to the various walled enclosures, the original scheme can be mentally reconstructed with ease with the aid of Kip's accurate delineation.

A bowling green was an invariable feature of a Queen Anne garden and was strongly advocated by J. James, who produced *The Theory and Practice of Gardening* in 1712. "A Bowling Green is one of the most agreeable Compartments of a Garden, and, when 'tis rightly placed, nothing is more pleasant to the Eye. It's hollow Figure covered with a beautiful Carpet of Turf very Smooth, and of a lively green, most commonly encompassed with a Row of tall Trees with Flower bearing shrubs, make a delightful composition, besides the Pleasure it afford us, of lying along its sloping Banks, in the shade, during the hottest weather."

That elaborate gardens were not exclusively confined to the houses of the great appears from Celia Fiennes' description of the fantasies at the Rectory at Banstead about 1700, "where the parson of the parish has diverted himself in his garden these fifty years, is now old and doates. His grass plotts has stones of divers fformes and sizes which he names Gods and Goddesses; and hedges and arbours of thorn soe neatly cut, and in all ffigures in great rounds. There are several heads painted wch are named Mogul Grand Seignior, Cham of Tartary, Zarr of Muscovy, placed in several places. Another Garden is Grass plotts with yews and holly Lawrells, round this on the bank is sett stones very thick, some very much bigger for officers, this is the whole Confederate army and their Generalls. Here is a trumpeter, Hercules and Bacchus and a hedge of Lawrell 7 fte broad."

Another Continental importation, but one that fortunately achieved little popularity in this country, was the "Practical Joke" water garden. There was an elaborate example at Wilton . . .

"A Grottoe is att ye end of the garden just ye middle off ye house—its garnished with many fine ffigures of ye Goddesses, and about 2 yards off the doore is severall pipes in a line that with a sluce spoutts water up to wett the strangers —in the middle roome is a round table and a large Pipe in the midst on which they put a Crown or Gun or a branch and so yt spouts the water through ye carvings and poynts all round the roome at ye Artists pleasure to wet ye company."

There were several other entertaining little contrivances of a similar nature, such as "figures that can weep water on the beholders" and a place where water descended in "a Shower of raine all about ye roome". But the most heartless was an ingenious arrangement whereby the water "makes ye melody of Nightingerlls and all sorts of birds". The simple stranger, already drenched but still naïvely enquiring, hurries to discover the origin of these entrancing sounds, but, alas, a "Sluce is moved" which "washes ye spectators designed for diversion". This was the end of the fun, and the delighted visitors could now return to the house for dinner.

At Chatsworth the gardens were more imaginative and less boisterous. There was every form of fountain. "There is one basin in the middle of one garden thats very large and by sluces beside the Images severall pipes plays out ye water —about 30 Large and small pipes altogether, some fflush it up that it ffrothes Like snow. . . ." In a walk stood "a fine willow tree, the Leaves, Barke and all looks very naturall, ye roote is full of rubbish or great stones to appearance and all on a sudden by turning a sluce it raines from Each Leafe and from the branches like a shower, it being made from Brass and pipes to Each Leafe", and there were several other fantasies. "On a little banck stands blew balls 10 on a side, and between each ball are 4 pipes wch. by a sluce spouts out water across ye stepps to Each other like an arbour or arch. This is designed to be Enlarged and steps made up to ye top of ye hill which is a vast ascent."

This latter scheme was subsequently carried out and still exists. The water rises from the summit of the dome of a classical temple which stands high on the wooded hill above the house, and descends in a long cascade formed by stone steps, to feed the fountains in the great sheet of water opposite the south façade of the house.

Although the most popular features of the Queen Anne garden were the statues and cut "greens", flowers and flowering shrubs were also grown, while in the bigger gardens orange and lemon trees in tubs were stood amongst the sculpture and the topiary work. The "greens" were very varied, and the observant Mrs. Fiennes noticed all sorts in Sir Thomas Patrells' "Grove", "ffirs, both silver, Scots, Norway, Cyprus, Yew, Bays etc." There were also "several squares being set full of these like a maze; they are compassed round Each square with a hedge of Lawrell about a yd high Cut exactly smooth and Even, there are also box trees in the middle".

Exotic plants were also imported into this country, and

122   THE VYNE, HAMPSHIRE : a Garden Pavilion (*circa* 1650)

123　STOKE BRUERNE PARK, NORTHAMPTONSHIRE : the Formal Pool.　The Pavilion is attributed to Inigo Jones

in the "Physick garden" at Oxford there were specimens kept under glass "ye aire being too rough for them". There were Aloes, and a Sensitive Plant "which curls up as if pained" when touched; there was also, most strange, "the humble plant that grows on a long slender Stalke and do but strike it, it falls flat on ye ground stalke and all, and after some time revives again and stands up".

Although formality in gardening was the fashion in the early years of the eighteenth century, the smaller houses were often surrounded by grounds of the most rustic simplicity. Mrs. Delany, in her Autobiography, described the surroundings of "The Farm", the home of her childhood of about 1716, which by no means subscribed to the fashionable form, yet nevertheless provided her with intense pleasure. "The front of the house faces the finest vale in England, the Vale of Evesham of which there is a very advantageous view from every window: the back part of the house is shaded by a very high hill which rises gradually: between lies the garden, a small spot of ground, but well stocked with fruit and ' flowers. Nothing could be more fragrant and rural: the sheep and cows came bleating and lowing to the pales of the garden. At some distance on the left was a rookery; on the right a little clear brook ran winding through a copse of young elms (the resort of many warbling birds), and fell with a cascade into the garden, completing the concert."

John Evelyn was an enthusiastic gardener and wrote several books on the subject. *Silva* dealt entirely with forest trees, but *Elysium Britannicum*, planned to cover every branch of horticulture, was never completed. He visited Lord Capel at his house at Kew and noted in his Diary that "his garden has the choicest fruit of any in England". He also much admired the oranges and myrtle in the green-houses. This garden was on the site of the present Kew Gardens, and, after Lord Capel's death, was taken by Frederick, Prince of Wales, who with his wife, Princess Augusta, kept up the horticultural traditions of the place. The prince and princess were enthusiasts indeed, and not only called in Kent to make structural improvements but also worked themselves and expected their reluctant friends to do likewise. Bubb Doddington recorded after a visit "all of us, men, women and children, worked on a new walk . . . a cold dinner". Sir William Chambers' pagoda and temples were erected a few years later during the years 1757–64, after the prince's death, when his widow was very much under the influence of Lord Bute, who was a keen horticulturist and had himself one of the finest gardens in England at Luton Hoo.

Very early in the eighteenth century the first stirrings of a reaction against the formal garden made themselves felt, and even Vanbrugh, hitherto an exponent of the architectural garden, urged the Duchess of Marlborough in 1707 to preserve the ruins of old Woodstock Manor in the park at Blenheim as it would "make one of the most agreeable objects that the best of landskip Painters can invent". The Duchess, however, did not share his feelings for the romantic, and the manor and its surrounding "greens" were destroyed.

This was the age of the painters of romantic landscape; Poussin, Panini, Salvator Rosa, Claude, were stimulating the imagination of the fashionable and artistic world.

> "O great Poussin! O Nature's darling, Claude!
> What if some rash and sacrilegious hand
> Tore from your canvass those umbrageous pines
> That frown in front, and give each azure hill
> The charm of contrast!"

So sang the Rev. William Mason, expressing in his own graceful lines the debt the new style owed to the landscape painter. It was a new notion to look on the garden as a picture:

> "Take thy plastic spade,
> It is thy pencil; take thy seeds, thy plants,
> They are thy colours; and by these repay
> With interest every charm she lent thy art."

Sentiment began to revolt against the rigid lines and angular restrictions which had been for so long the vogue, and welcomed the untrammelled freedom of the picturesque manner. Professional garden makers soon developed schemes for remodelling the formal surroundings of country houses into faint copies of the canvasses which found such favour on Palladian walls. Seldom could the mild English country be so transformed as to assume something of the dramatic or sublime; occasionally, however, there were exceptions, as at Hawkstone in Shropshire, where even the unemotional Dr. Johnson was shaken out of his calm "by the extent of its prospects, the awfulness of its shades, the horror of its precipices, the verdure of its hollows, and the loftiness of its rocks. The ideas which it forces upon the mind are the sublime, the dreadful and the vast. Above is inaccessible altitude, below is horrible profundity."

124 BLENHEIM PALACE, OXFORDSHIRE: the Entrance to the Stable Court. Begun in 1705; Sir John Vanbrugh, Architect

125 GLYNDE, SUSSEX: the 18th-Century Stable Arch

126 WILTON HOUSE, WILTSHIRE : the Palladian Bridge across
the Nadder. Designed by Robert Morris, *circa* 1750

127 WESTBURY COURT, GLOUCESTERSHIRE : the late
17th-Century Water Garden

William Kent was one of the earliest to lay out gardens in the landscape manner, but his schemes were something of a compromise; avenues and formal plantations were in juxtaposition to winding paths through groves and wildernesses; but of flowers or parterres there was no trace. Indeed flowers, which had been so popular during the seventeenth century and the early years of the eighteenth, seem now to have lost their appeal, and the few that were grown were planted within the walled kitchen gardens so that no discordant note of colour could disturb the simple verdure of the grounds.

Kent's most famous garden was at Chiswick Villa, where he laid out an elaborate scheme of avenues and groves for Lord Burlington, with broad paths leading away from the house to a circular pond, on the edge of which was a graceful temple, said to have been "the first essay of his Lordship's happy invention". Again to quote the enthusiastic Rev. Mason:

"Kent who felt
The pencil's power: but fir'd by higher forms
Of beauty than that pencil knew to paint,
Work'd with the living hues that Nature lent,
And realiz'd his landscapes . . . "

Topiary work in yew or box fell into disfavour, and "the mournful family of Yews" is disparagingly mentioned by Alexander Pope, who also "touches upon the ill taste of those who are so fond of *Evergreens* (particularly yews which are the most tonsile) as to destroy the nobler Forest-trees, to make way for such little Ornaments, as Pyramids of dark green continually repeated, not unlike a funeral procession". In his *Epistle to Lord Burlington*, no doubt with Kent's work in mind, the same writer explains the new theory for laying out the surroundings of a house: that instead of drilling the gardens into that strict formality which had hitherto been thought indispensable, the natural conformations of the ground should be moulded and improved upon, and full advantage taken of every mound or dell. "The first Rule to adapt all to the *Nature* and *Use* of the *Place*, and the beauties not forced into, but resulting from it."

He then expands this rule in verse:

"To build, to plant, whatever you intend,
To rear the Column, or the Arch to bend,
To swell the Terras, or to sink the Grot;
In all, let *Nature* never be forgot.

Q

But treat the Goddess like a modest fair,
Nor overdress, nor leave her wholly bare;
Let not each beauty ev'rywhere be spy'd,
Where half the skill is decently to hide;
He gains all points, who pleasingly confounds,
Surprizes, varies, and conceals the Bounds.
    Consult the *Genius* of the place in all;
That tells the waters or to rise, or fall,
Or helps th' ambitious Hill the heav'n to scale,
Or scoops in circling Theatres the Vale,
Calls in the country, catches opening glades,
Joins willing woods, and varies shades from shades,
Now breaks, or now directs, th' intending Lines,
Paints as you plant, and as you work, designs
    Begin with *Sense*, of ev'ry Art the soul,
Parts answering parts shall slide into a whole,
Spontaneous beauties all around advance,
Start ev'n from Difficulty, strike from Chance."

The penultimate line expresses most succinctly the essence of
the landscape theory of gardening. But groves and glades,
unbroken sweeps of turf and sheets of water did not comprise
the perfect park without a classical temple or two, an obelisk
or an arch placed on some suitable eminence to give that
touch of the artificial which so enhanced the natural beauty
of the prospect.

The most famous landscape layout of the period was at
Stowe in Buckinghamshire, where Lord Cobham, during the
first half of the eighteenth century, planted his undulating
park in consonance with the new approved taste and added
to the charms of Nature by erecting pavilions, monuments,
pillars, obelisks and also a large number of temples dedicated
to a variety of patrons. There were Temples of Concord
and Victory, of Venus, of the British Worthies; there was
the Boycott Pavilion; a Rotunda; the Queen's Building; a
Palladian bridge similar to that at Wilton; an obelisk over
100 feet high to the memory of General Wolfe; the Congreve
Monument. The majority of these were designed by Kent.
In addition there was a pillar designed by Gibbs over 115 feet
high, surmounted by a statue of Lord Cobham. Little wonder
that Pope should write: "If anything under Paradise could
set me beyond earthly objects, Stowe might do it." A century
later, however, taste had changed, and the gardens had been
largely remodelled by Capability Brown, who had nevertheless retained many of the temples and obelisks. Prince Pückler-
Muskau, visiting the place in 1826, did not share Pope's

enthusiasm. "The grounds were laid out long ago, and though in many respects beautiful, and remarkable for fine lofty trees, are so overloaded with temples, and buildings of all sorts, that the greatest possible improvement to the place would be the pulling down of ten or a dozen of them."

At Stourhead in Wiltshire a less elaborate but more exquisite scene was created by Mr. Henry Hoare who had bought the estate in 1714. The water from six springs, forming the source of the river Stour, was gathered together and brought underground to a grotto, whence it poured from under the recumbent figure of a nymph into a vast artificial lake surrounded by rhododendrons and hanging beech woods amongst which were placed three graceful classical temples. Most fortunately the beauties of Stourhead have been carefully preserved, and it remains one of the most romantic places in the country.

The classical preoccupation was often carried to ridiculous extremes, especially in small gardens, where temples and statues were particularly unsuitable. Mrs. Pendarves (later Delany) writing in 1733 gives an example:

> "In the garden is a fir grove dedicated to Venus, in the midst of which is her statue, at some distance from it is a mound covered with evergreens, on which is placed a temple with a statue of Apollo. Neptune, Proserpine, Diana, all have due honours paid them, and Fame has been too good a friend to the master of all these improvements to be neglected; *her* temple is near the house, at the end of a terrace, near which the four Seasons take their stand, very well represented by Flora, Ceres, Bacchus, and an old gentleman with a hood on his head warming his hands over a fire."

This light-hearted paganism, however, was more agreeable than the Protestant fervour of the eccentric old gentleman of Newton Burgsland who, in the early years of the nineteenth-century, decorated his garden with "mounds covered by sweet smelling flowers in memory of the Graves of Protestant Martyrs and Reformers".

The classical was not the only style for garden temples. At Taplow Court there was "a Gothic Roothouse which hangs pendant over the river. The inside is Gothic paper resembling stucco; the upper part being painted glass, gives a pleasing gloom."

A pleasing gloom, an agreeable melancholy, these were sentiments which the late eighteenth century landscape gardeners endeavoured to inspire, and which, with the willing aid of romantic-natured visitors, they were often able to induce. A ruined bower, a winding brook, a wooded glade were more than enough to send the delighted visitor into ecstasies of romantic melancholy. And should they by chance visit some spot where nature was indeed in a wild mood their transports knew no bounds.

A rare, but vastly admired, addition to the romantic interest of a garden was the provision of a Hermit's Cave, complete with an "Ornamental Hermit". An economical method of securing this interesting object was to arrange a stuffed figure in a suitable costume, which could be vaguely distinguished by the dim light of a lantern, poring over his book and hour-glass in the deepest recesses of some awful grotto; but occasionally some poor creature was paid to fill this melancholy role. Mr. Hamilton at Pain's Hill in Surrey secured a hermit who was to "continue in the hermitage seven years, where he should be provided with a Bible, optical glasses, a mat for his feet, a hassock for his pillow, an hourglass for his timepiece, water for his beverage, and food from the house. He must wear a camlet robe, and never, under any circumstances, must he cut his hair, beard, or nails, stray beyond the limits of Mr. Hamilton's grounds, or exchange one word with the servants!" But, alas, though a hermit was easy to secure he was more difficult to retain, and Mr. Hamilton's recluse returned to the world at the end of three weeks.

As has already been observed, Kent was one of the first to break away from the rigid French and Dutch styles of gardening, but Lancelot Brown, known as Capability (1715–1783) was to become the most famous figure of the landscape school. He started life as a gardener in the employ of Lord Cobham at Stowe, but his talents in landscape gardening soon brought him to a wider sphere. Following at first in the footsteps of Kent, he adopted far more drastic methods. All patterns and formal beds were swept away; avenues were so decimated as to appear as haphazard groups of trees rather than as hard and serried lines, a process known as "clumping an avenue"; and round or rectangular pools were converted into simple sheets of water looking, as far as possible, as if provided rather by benevolent Nature than by the artifice of man. In a few years all over England "the obdurate and straight line of the Dutch was softened into a curve, the terrace melted into a swelling bank and the walks opened to catch the vicinal country". And as it is so admirably expressed in *The Gentleman's House*, "the Palladian basin, with its severe geometrical form, has become an irregular Lake, with stray arms bending behind bushy promontories and meeting round little islets of trees; and the underground conduits by which our grandfathers would have supplied and relieved it, are open streamlets, meandering waywardly over whatever variety of bed the artist can command". Crowning some nearby hill would be the inevitable crumbling Gothic ruin in the shape of a tower or arch, often forming, such was the practical sense beneath this romantic spirit, one side of a gamekeeper's cottage.

A contemporary couplet neatly expresses the influence of the romantic painters on this taste.

"At Blenheim, Croome and Caversham we trace
Salvator's wildness, Claude's enlivening grace. . . . "

And the Rev. Mason included a little panegyric in his poem on the English Garden:

"Bards yet unborn
Shall pay to Brown that tribute, fitliest paid
In strains, the beauty of his scenes inspire."

The sweeping away of formal gardens must have created an immense economy in upkeep, but the moulding of the ground to provide the most picturesque effect often entailed considerable expense. Not only were groves of trees planted and streams dammed to give the appearance of broad and winding rivers, but occasionally, in order to obtain a glimpse of a distant prospect, a shallow valley would be boldly cut through an intervening slope, as was done at Charborough Park in Dorset; or an offending village would be bodily transported, as at Kedleston, where a large number of cottages and an inn, which was much patronised by those who came to drink the salubrious waters which rise in the park, were pulled down and re-erected at a more respectful distance from the house, so that the eye could wander over the wide and verdant stretches of the park without encountering any object so menial as a cottage. With the appearance, however, a few years later, of the *cottage orné* this prejudice against a glimpse of the poor declined.

Few were as fortunate in obtaining free labour as Lady Hester Stanhope, who, having heard her uncle William Pitt

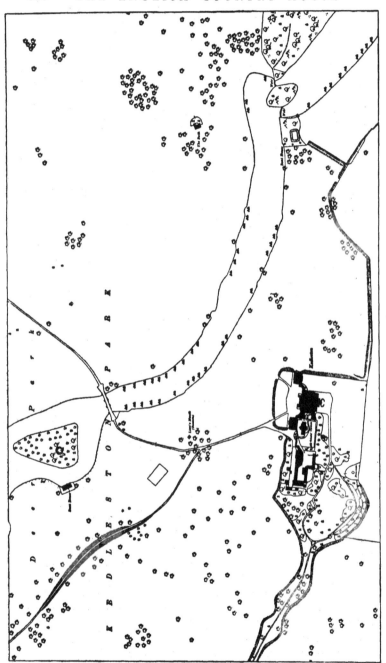

KEDLESTON, DERBYSHIRE: HOUSE, CHURCH, GARDEN AND PARK

say that Walmer Castle needed a better setting, took the opportunity of his absence in 1805 to make material improvements to the garden. "I got, I know not how", she wrote, "all the regiments that were in quarters at Dover, and I employed them in levelling, fetching turf, transplanting shrubs, flowers etc. . . . a few civil words and occasionally a present, made the work go on rapidly and it was finished before Mr. Pitt's return." Pitt was delighted with the result and congratulated her on keeping "to the old manner of avenues, alleys and the like" as most suitable to an ancient castle.

Another, but less extreme exponent of the landscape school was Humphrey Repton (1752–1818). He had adopted the profession of landscape-gardener in a desperate effort to recoup his losses on his scheme for improving the conveyance of letters, and eventually made a considerable fortune in this less hazardous employment. He clearly stated his own attitude towards the rival claims of the formal and the picturesque. "I do not profess to follow either Le Notre or Brown, but selecting beauties from the style of each, to adopt so much of the grandure of the former as may accord with a palace, and so much of the grace of the latter as may call forth the charms of the natural landscape. Each has its proper situation; and good taste will make fashion subservient to good sense." Thus, while he carried on something of the tradition of Capability Brown, he had milder views on the placing of such necessary adjuncts to a house as the kitchen garden. He preferred that it should be discreetly concealed by trees, but did not demand its banishment to some distant part of the park. And within its walls he advocated the cultivation of flowers, a practice entirely neglected by Brown.

His first great work was at Cobham Hall in Kent, where he altered the gardens and planted the park about 1790 very much after the manner of Capability Brown; but as the years went on he came to feel a greater enthusiasm for gardens, so that at Ashridge, which he calls "the child of my age and declining powers", the garden layout assumed an elaboration which would have been anathema to Brown. There was, indeed, no formality, but winding paths led through deep groves of trees, bringing the visitor to such hidden points of interest as the Broad Sanctuary and Holy Well, Pomarium and Winter Walk, the Monks' Garden (130), the Arboretum of exotic trees, the Magnolia and American Garden, the Embroidered Parterre, Grotto, Cabinet de Verdure, Rosarium and Fountain.

Here was the first step towards the gardens of the Victorians.

A favourite feature of interest in a late eighteenth-century garden was a menagerie or aviary, which was often architecturally constructed but seldom contained anything wilder than some exotic birds. In 1769 Mrs. Lybbe Powys visited the Duchess Dowager of Portland's menagerie at Bulstrode, which contained "a curassoa, goon, crown-bird, stork, black and red game, bustards, red-legged partridges, silver, gold, pied pheasants one, what is reckon'd exceedingly curious, the peacock-pheasant". There was also an aviary in which was "a most beautiful collection of smaller birds—tumblers, waxbills, yellow and bloom paraquets, Java sparrows, Loretta blue birds, Virginia nightingales, and two widow-birds, or, as Edward calls them, 'red breasted long twit'd finches '."

Some years later she visited Osterley Park but was very disappointed by the menagerie "which fell far short of my expectation, that of Lady Ailesbury at Park Place is vastly superior in elegance". But the most elaborate aviary of all was at Temple, near Marlow, where, "at the end of a most magnificent greenhouse is an aviary full of all kinds of birds flying loose in a large octagon of gilt wire, in which is a fountain in the centre, and in the evening tis illuminated by wax-lights, while the water falls down some rock-work in form of a cascade. This has a pretty effect but seems to alarm its beautiful inhabitants, and must be cold for them I should imagine."

In 1827 Pückler-Muskau, visiting Wentworth Woodhouse in Yorkshire, noticed "an inclosure made of wire fence, running along the gay parterres, peopled with foreign birds, a clear brook flowing through it, and planted with evergreens, on which the feathered inhabitants could sport at pleasure". And at Woburn there was an extremely elaborate example, in which each rare bird "had his own dwelling and little garden. These birds' houses were made of twigs interwoven with wire, the roof also of wire, the shrubs around evergreen. As we walked out upon the open space which occupies the centre, our Papageno whistled, and in an instant the air was literally darkened around us by flights of pigeons, chickens, and heaven knows what birds."

The sixth Duke of Devonshire had a rather more alarming taste in pets. It appears from the letters of his sister, Countess Granville, that he kept at Chiswick, in addition to a herd of deer, "a few kangaroos, who if affronted will rip up anyone

128 WREST PARK, BEDFORDSHIRE : the Canal and Temple
(mid-18th Century)

129 KEDLESTON, DERBYSHIRE. A late 18th-Century Garden Urn.

130 ASHRIDGE PARK, HERTFORDSHIRE: the Monks' Garden,
designed by Humphrey Repton, *circa* 1810

131 IN THE SALISBURY CLOSE: an 18th-Century Gate and Piers

as soon as look at him, elks, emus, and other pretty sportive death-dealers playing about". And again: "The lawn was beautifully variegated by an Indian bull and his spouse, and goats of all colours and dimensions." In 1828 Sir Walter Scott, when visiting Chiswick, was astonished to see a female elephant wandering up and down in the charge of a groom.

The early years of the nineteenth century were rather barren of new ideas in gardens, and P. F. Robinson's *Designs for Farm Buildings*, which appeared in 1830, was received with some enthusiasm. He aimed at introducing a cosmopolitan note into the English country; besides designs for old English cottages, monastic barns and rustic cow-houses, which can be infinitely beautified by allowing "Virginian creeper, Periploca or trailing Arbutus partially to climb the side and hang from the roof", there are Swiss Barns, French Cottages, Italian Dovecotes and Smithies, a Circular Granary "which seen from the adjoining plantation would remind the traveller of the Temple of Venus at Naples, the roof assuming the form of the Temple of Vesta". But perhaps the most striking design is that for a Reservoir "composed after the celebrated Lighthouse at Genoa" which the author was convinced would "introduce into the landscape a distinguished object as seen from the adjacent hills".

The Rustic Seat would be a necessary feature of the Plantation Walk leading to the Farmyard or Dairy. It could be decorated with twisted branches, while all other woodwork was painted to represent oak, and the floor "may be finished in imitation of a tessellated pavement, by branches only, forming a dry and comfortable bottom".

Robinson was a great admirer of the writing of Sir Uvedale Price and quotes his views on the importance of making use of any picturesque building to form a romantic feature in the landscape—"in mills particularly, such is the extreme intricacy of the wheels and the woodwork, such the singular variety of form and of light and shadow, of mosses and weather stains from the constant moisture, of plants springing from the rough joints of the stones; such the assemblage of everything which most conduces to the picturesque, that even without the addition of water an old mill has the greatest charm for a painter".

Robinson suggests further improvements to this romantic picture by the addition of a Rustic Bridge. "An old tree, thrown across the stream, with a rude handrail formed by a branch of ash, is generally preferable to any regular design."

R

The rustic summer or root-house became a favourite objective for a walk. Prince Pückler-Muskau, on his travels through England, came across a "curious *pavillion rustic* which is built in a suitable spot in the 'pleasure ground'. It is hexagonal, three sides solid, and fashioned of pieces of rough branches of trees very prettily arranged in various patterns, the other three consisted of two windows and a door. The floor is covered with a mosaic of little pebbles from the brook, the ceiling with shells, and the roof is thatched with wheat straw, on which the full ears are left." A few days later he found another which "had just been covered with purple heather. A less happy thought was a stuffed tiger, lying as if alive in the ante-room."

Mr. Robinson's cultivated designs may, on the rare occasions when they were carried out, have added to the interest of park and landscape, but it was the garden which at this period and for the following half-century was most in need of constructive assistance. Repton brought back the garden to popularity, and his successors developed his ideals from the point at which they were left at his death in 1818. But those enticing paths which Repton had wound, apparently so purposefully, through his obscuring groves now lost their object, and were apt to meander meaninglessly about great lawns with nothing to control their direction but an occasional group of laurel or other dreary shrub. Specimen conifers were planted at regular intervals on vast expanses of mown grass, and, should greater grandeur be required, a few more acres were enclosed from the park and similarly treated. The essential architectural relationship between house and garden was entirely neglected.

By 1827 Kent's romantic vistas at Chiswick Villa, which must then have been in their prime, were being destroyed to make way for the bleak new fashion "now prevalent in England, of planting the 'pleasure-ground' with single trees or shrubs placed at a considerable distance, almost in rows. . . . This gives the grass-plots the air of nursery grounds. The shrubs are trimmed round so as not to touch each other, the earth carefully cleared about them every day, and the edges of the turf cut into stiff lines, so that you see more of black earth than of green foliage, and the free beauty of nature is quite checked."

And this uninspired version of the landscape style was to be the vogue during the major part of Queen Victoria's reign. Interest was concentrated on flowers, layout was neglected. The grand manner had been lost with the eighteenth century; more and more, gardens tended to become a collection of unrelated details, without any general controlling plan. Only in horticulture was there a real advance. New plants were brought into the country from all over the world, and at Kew and elsewhere were improved and developed beyond recognition. In 1833 Nathaniel Ward published *The Growth of Plants in Closely-Glazed Cases*, which demonstrated the great benefits to be obtained by the use of a greenhouse, and in 1840 Paxton built the vast conservatory at Chatsworth, recently demolished, which was to provide the inspiration for the Crystal Palace. Greenhouses became general, and the production of flowers was infinitely improved, both in variety and quality. Soon the amorphous Victorian lawns were enlivened with brilliant patches of carpet-bedding, and the scarlet geranium, the yellow calceolaria, the bright blue lobelia provided a riot of contrasting colours of which nineteenth-century gardeners seem never to have tired.

Towards the end of the century, however, the bleak lawn with specimen trees began to pall, and enterprising gardeners turned back to the past for inspiration. Once again the French and Italian styles came into fashion, and gardens, from being bleak and dull, became fussy and overloaded with ornament and detail; only with the present century, so one likes to think, has that just alliance of interesting detail, coupled with broad and simple lines, untrammelled by particular style or fashion, been achieved.

INDEX

(The numerals in italic type denote the *figure numbers* of illustrations.)

Lightning Source UK Ltd.
Milton Keynes UK
UKHW040916230119
336024UK00020B/32/P

9 781445 511771

Lightning Source UK Ltd.
Milton Keynes UK
UKHW040916230119
336024UK00020B/32/P